MW00426163

# MUSINGS

*from the*

# HEIGHTS

*An anthology of reflections*
*on the Christian life for Seekers,*
*Pilgrims and Overcomers*

# J. R. MOLINA

© 2018 José R. Molina
Published by Smith Beach Press

ISBN: 978-1731239891
LCCN:

Editing by Debbie Maxwell Allen

Cover by Shayne Rutherford
WWW.WICKEDGOODBOOKCOVERS.COM

Interior by Colleen Sheehan
WWW.AMPERSANDBOOKINTERIORS.COM

Smith Beach Press

# CONTENTS

# DEDICATIONS

I DEDICATE THIS BOOK (my second published work) to the Summerall Chapel community at The Citadel, the Military College of South Carolina where I have the privilege to serve as their Chaplain and Director of Religious Activities. Their unrelenting hunger for truth inspires and emboldens me to "Preach the word…in season and out of season" (2Timothy 4:2). I am thankful for the freedom I experience in boldly proclaiming and teaching the Scriptures in their midst. May our Lord continue to bless and direct their vision for service as they worship The Most High.

I also dedicate this work to the Fisher House Foundation, Inc. (https://www.fisherhouse.org). This book is made available to you for free. (no personal royalties to the author). If you accept this free gift, I only ask that you make a tax-exempt gift to the Fisher House. The Fisher House Foundation is a nonprofit organization dedicated to providing temporary lodging and transportation expenses used for those families with military service members who are convalescing at military and civilian hospitals throughout the United States. The Foundation also awards scholarships for qualified children of military service members.

# ACKNOWLEDGMENTS

*✛ I have not stopped giving thanks for you, remembering you in my prayers.*

*(Ephesians 1:16)*

I AM CONVINCED THAT nothing happens by accident. Our friendships, our spouse, our kids, our teachers and mentors have all entered our lives with a providential purpose. Therefore, giving thanks is an easy thing when we realize that our accomplishments are not our own. Our attainments are really the sum of the emotional and spiritual investments that others have made along the way. It is in this spirit that I wish to give thanks.

I am so very grateful to my wife Vicky for the unconditional love and support that she expresses to me in her own gentle and quiet fashion. Truly, her love resembles the love of our Lord in so many ways. To my beloved sons, Tommy and Danny, who bring great joy to my heart. Their love, playfulness and respect bring thankful pause to my life when I need it most.

A word of thanks to my dear brother in the Lord, Master Chief Harry Terry (United States Navy, retired) who enthusiastically encouraged me (more than once) to compile this collection of essays.

A special expression of thanks to a mentor, the Reverend Daniel Yeary, who many years ago saw my potential to serve God vocationally and deposited in me a legacy of teaching and preaching which continue to fuel my passion for the pulpit ministry of the church.

I'm most grateful for the invaluable teaching ministry of the Reverend, Dr. RC Sproul (1939-2017). This world-class scholar, theologian and seminary professor engaged me in some of the most rigorous and joyful learning experiences in my seminary formation. He could fathom the depths and yet maintain a practical grip on reality and application

Finally, my brother in the faith, the Rev. David Thatcher Wilson. His unrelenting faith, ministry of presence and commitment to the Glorious Gospel have kept me accountable and inspired. It is through his good offices, as Director of Smith Beach Press, that this work is made possible, for the Glory of God. Look up David's numerous and engaging published works on Amazon.

The author of Ecclesiastes expressed a great truism: *Of making many books there is no end.... (12:12)* Indeed, many better books by much more gifted authors have preceded and are sure to follow this one. However, none will ever surpass the transcendent excellence and beauty of the most popular book in the history of mankind, for *All Scripture is God-breathed and is useful for teaching, rebuking, correcting and training in righteousness, so that the man of God may be thoroughly equipped for every good work. (2 Timothy 3:16-17)*

## How to Use this Book

THE BOOK IS organized topically, identifying the different phases in the journey of faith from the nascent questions posed by those seeking to know God up through the ultimate questions at the end of life. These essays represent a collection of sermon summaries and personal reflections that encompass thirty years in vocational ministry and seek to address areas of practical life-application. Consequently, the readings in this book can be used in a variety of ways, as follows:

1.  The book can be read by anyone investigating the Christian faith and desiring to understand how that faith fleshes-out in the practical areas of life, thought and work.

2.  For the Christian, the book can be utilized for personal devotional readings. The essays can also supplement any personal daily reading plan. In this way, each reflection can be read separately as the reader identifies with a particular topic.

3.  The book's topical organization can make it a handy referencing tool for use in small group discussions or to supplement Bible study curriculum that may address any one of the book's topics.

4.  As a tool for giving advice and encouragement, the topical essays can be shared with friends, family and acquaintances that may be traversing comparable scenarios in their lives.

5.  The beginner or experienced homilist can utilize the various articles to illustrate points as they engage their congregations in practical scriptural application.

# PREFACE

⊹ *In the long tradition of the liberal arts, words are the tools employed for sculpting the lineaments of culture upon the human soul. ...What distinguishes man from animal, said the ancients, is the use of words.*[1]

WORDS ARE IMPORTANT! A scholarly aunt was the first to impress me with the inherent power of words. From earliest childhood I was taught to love and respect books as one might a good friend. To be sure, I grew to love books and cannot imagine living life without them. Answers were to be found in books, so I learned, for books are the repository for the collective wisdom of the ages. The message was then reinforced through an educational journey carefully orchestrated by a host of teachers and mentors that confirmed the power of words.

So, it was only normal that I would turn to books when I started to contemplate the ultimate questions of life. Why do I live now and not in another era? What am I here for? What is the purpose of my life? If my life has purpose, what is its end? Is there an afterlife? The questions came as I traversed a difficult time as a young adult. Through a personal crisis of self doubt I gravitated from

---

1    Samuel T. Logan, Jr. (Ed), *The Preacher and Preaching* (Phillipsburg, NJ: Presbyterian Publishing Co., 1986) 303.

having book knowledge about God to an indolent type of agnosticism, bordering on atheism. It was apathetic because I became oblivious to the possibility of God's existence and refused to engage in dialogue, debate or significant personal reflection. After all, if God did not exist why bother arguing the point? Consequently, I lived my life as a "functional" atheist.

However, this godless existence had its repercussions and as the noose of self-doubt tightened in my life I continued to seek out the answer in books. That's where Barnes and Nobles Booksellers enter the picture. I was living in New York City at the time and walked into B & N's multi-story, main store and asked the sales attendant for a Bible. Well, the salesman gave me an odd look – the type of look a salesperson would give an "atypical" customer. Still, I was dead serious. He then asked, "Which version would you like?" The question threw me for a loop. What version? As far as I was concerned there was only one Bible. Indeed, there is only one Bible. That is, the clerk was asking which translation I preferred. I honestly answered that I did not know and asked him to recommend a version. He played it safe (conservative) and sold me a King James Version. The Bible! I had never read it cover-to-cover. Surely, this revered book had to contain some information that might address my search for truth (of the ultimate kind) if it could be found.

As I commenced to read, the answers did not come quickly (and I still have unanswered questions). However, little did I know that my life had started on a new journey and that in time I would come to know of the certainty of God's existence and The Almighty's eternal love for us. Little did I suspect that through this marvelous book I would meet God's Son and embrace Jesus' invitation to a relationship with Him (of the eternal kind). But after all, in the words of Rick Warren's Purpose Driven Life, "It's not about you."[2] This is about the power of words, particularly God's Word, that can change lives and reorient entire societies through its transformative message. Holy Scripture, whether it appears in written, oral forms or the arts, continues to exert influence to change lives, impact society and shape its culture. To be sure, one cannot separate the history of western civilization from the history of the Bible and Christendom. In modern times, who can dismiss the efforts of the late Dr. Martin Luther King and his masterful application of the spoken word, in general, and The Bible in particular, as he lead the modern civil rights movement and changed the course of American History?

Integral to this process is the role played by the Christian message in effectively communicating to our contemporary pluralistic society. I am fascinated, even intrigued, by the inherent power and authority vested in the "Word" in communicating the claims of the historic Christian faith. Christians claim to possess divinely revealed propositional truth that addresses the very meaning of life, answering man's deepest longing for transcendent truth. This worldview contends that the living God desires to redeem all of creation through His incarnate son, Jesus Christ and in so doing extend the gift of eternal life to all men.

Our modern pluralistic "landscape" has brought together assorted groups that possess a diversity of worldview stories. This contemporary environment poses both a challenge and an opportunity to enter the marketplace of ideas and engage in the dialogue, with gentleness and respect. For some Christians this current state of affairs may represent an unsurpassable obstacle. However, I concur with those who, instead, see an invaluable opportunity to

---

2    Rick Warren, *The Purpose Driven Life (Grand Rapids, MI: Zondervan, 2002) 17.*

communicate the Gospel and show that the Christian faith is reasonable, believable and practical. It is through words that the Christian worldview enters this arena of diverse ideas. In this milieu of opinions and contending narratives, impressions are made, and movements are born within society. The possibilities for effecting positive change become incalculable!

Certainly, this will demand our very best creative efforts. The potential for success is great, but people of faith must be prepared to engage in the mainstream of the communication process in all its applications. Yes, this means becoming consummate students of the Christian faith. In time successful engagement will be determined by how well we have intelligently and skillfully utilized the vehicles of communication at our reach.

Christian literature must seek to examine, interpret and critique with robust clarity the dilemmas faced by contemporary society and then present the answers offered by the Christian worldview with the love and hope that only Christ can offer.

Theological research must continue to address with integrity the deepest questions posed by mankind. Our scholars must open themselves to the honest questions and critique of seekers and the scholarly community at large.

The arts must excel in expressing the beauty and grandeur that is representative of an infinite and majestic God.

Social initiatives must equip the underprivileged and the displaced in our society with the tools necessary to build their lives and in so doing manifest the God of mercies who works dynamically through the lives of his people.

I have a Christian friend who is an attorney. Through this friend I learned that being a Christian and an attorney does not violate the law of non-contradiction. He once shared with me that whenever litigating a case he always sought to walk the "high ground."

That is, he based his professional ethic on Jesus' Sermon on the Mount. He maintained that if he could walk the high ground and not stoop to the "low ground" of questionable motives and ethical turpitude, God would honor his efforts. I would add, and he would agree, that walking the high ground and then holding it is not an easy thing (but neither is it impossible). Holding the high ground takes daily commitment, dedication, humility and a tenacity that is born of God's grace as we consistently seek that grace. It is my hope that this collection of personal reflections on the spiritual life will enrich your journey as your imagination and thoughts are engaged and challenged.

Dr. Joe Molina, D.Min, (Charleston, SC, August 4, 2018)

*⭻* *For the word of God is living and active. Sharper than any double-edged sword, it penetrates even to dividing soul and spirit, joints and marrow; it judges the thoughts and attitudes of the heart.*
*(Hebrews 4:12)*

# INTRODUCTION

## WORDS DO COUNT

I THINK I'M SAFE in making the following observation: Most people have an interest in a person's dying words. Please, don't misunderstand! I don't mean a morbid or gossipy curiosity. In fact, it's very possible that we may experience a sense of reverence when witnessing and hearing those last words. We want to capture the significance of those words. After all, we'll never hear that person's voice again and we want to embrace the final thoughts those words express. To be sure, last words may reflect a person's first priorities. History has taught us that:

DRUMMER BUDDY RICH died after surgery in 1987. As he was being prepped for surgery, a nurse asked him, "Is there anything you can't take?" Rich replied, "Yeah, country music." *

BLUES SINGER BESSIE SMITH died saying, "I'm going, but I'm going in the name of the Lord." *

FAMOUS CHURCHMAN CHARLES WESLEY simply said, "Satisfied."

---

*   http://mentalfloss.com/article/58534/64-people-and-
    their-famous-last-words, Chris Higgins

*Adonirum Judson*: This incomparable missionary and statesman said as follows: "When the Lord calls, I shall go home with the gladness of a boy bounding away from school!"

Indeed, words have not only steered the course of history but have been used either to uplift or undermine individual lives. Let's face it; words are important whether they are spoken or written. The words that come out of our mouths mirror our thoughts. If I may quote an adage: "Out of the abundance of the heart, the mouth speaks." This is a sobering reality. Whether we believe it or not, the words we speak can enhance life or undermine it. Our words determine outcomes of events and identify who we are. We simply cannot ignore this. Knowing this, how do we individually measure up? Consider the following questions:

1. Do our words generally help or hurt others?
2. Do our words reveal or hide who we are?
3. Do our words manipulate or seek to entrap?
4. Do our words empower others to live good lives?
5. Do our words express encouragement or do our words reflect emptiness?
6. Are our words the same whether the person we are talking about is absent or present?

These can be difficult questions but of critical importance in measuring who we are as persons. With our mouths (or with our pens) we can speak words of life or words of discouragement. Some of the most famous last words in history were uttered about 2000 years ago by a young Palestinian Jew while being executed on a Roman cross. His words revolutionized the world's perspective of God and created a new hope for eternity. While impaled on that cross Jesus of Nazareth uttered seven statements. Among those statements were declarations of forgiveness (we all need to experience forgiveness) and words of eternal hope (we all need hope, especially of the eternal variety). He made a choice to speak words of *life*.

We, my friends, can choose to speak words of life. Speak words of life and watch the results!

# SECTION I
## IF TRUTH BE KNOWN

*⊹* *The heavens declare the glory of God; the skies proclaim the work of his hands...*
  *Their voice goes out into all the earth, their
words to the ends of the world.*
                    *(Psalm19: verses 1&4)*

## WHAT'S TRUE NORTH? (ON GOD'S EXISTENCE)

How MANY OF you believe that there is such a thing as "true north"? Can you close your eyes and point to it? How do you know that there is a true north? You know that there is such a thing because it is based on true principles of natural law. Would true north exist whether you existed or not? Absolutely! Its existence is not contingent on your personal existence. Well, let me "lighten up" a little. A certain student brought home a report card with questionable grades in 2 subject areas. When confronted by her parents and asked why she had not done well, the six-year-old quickly replied: "...because I had the hiccups" (clever but wrong).

The low grades were a consequence of not grasping the truth of the subject matter. Therefore, the student had not tested well.

How do you know that God Exists? Some might say that the primary reason for religion is because man is afraid and therefore needs to invent God as a security blanket. Sigmund Freud once speculated that fear of nature causes man to invent God. Freud claimed that the need for belief in God is psychological, biased and not to be trusted.

My response to all this is that I, Joe Molina, desperately wants God to exist. If I could be convinced, beyond any shadow of doubt that God doesn't exist I would find life to be the absurdity of absurdities. Life would be devoid of any ultimate significance. But still, my desperate need for God's existence is not a good enough answer. My opinion cannot establish God's existence no more than unicorns exist because I desperately want them to exist. I believe that God exists because natural law points to that existence. I believe that God exists because that same natural law informs me that God is "that being than which a greater being cannot be conceived" (Anselm of Canterbury). God is the perfection of perfections. I can't conceive nor think of anything or anyone more perfect and, to boot, God's handiwork of design is all over natural law.

God, then, is "true north," if you will. God, then, is the true reference point and that reference point is observable all around us through the order, the power, the control and detailed design that have been displayed in God's creation. Can all this be a product of pure, random accident? I submit to you that anything which is randomly accidental in nature is innately irrational. That which is irrational can never create a design that is innately rational. As Albert Einstein put it, "God doesn't roll dice."

As we observe and study the design we can notice that natural law is dynamic, constantly changing and constantly moving. So, who initiated the whole thing into motion anyway? Well, I believe you have to go way back and start with the "unmoved mover." The unmoved mover is the one being who initiated the motion. I identify this author of the motion as "God."

God, the cosmological author, would still exist whether I existed or not. God's existence is not predicated on my existence. Rather, my existence is totally grounded on God's existence. I have a suspicion that many may even have a greater need to disprove and dispose of God's existence. Why? Well, if I can prove that God doesn't exist then there is no ultimate personal accountability. God's non-existence can become a convenient accommodation. If there is no God then I can create my own convenient and strictly temporary distractions. *The fool says in his heart, 'there is no God'. (Psalm 14:1)*

✙ *But if…you seek the Lord your God, you will find Him if you seek Him with all your heart and with all your soul.*

*(Deuteronomy 4:29)*

## IF YOU SEEK WITH ALL YOUR HEART

HAVE YOU TAKEN a moment recently to notice your neighbor's ears? Have you paid close attention to the size and shape? Is one bigger than the other? I'm asking because there's an interesting theory (not) in circulation that claims that it is possible to judge a person's personality by the shape of his/her ears. Wow! What a position to be in! Just by looking at ears you can know what makes that person tick. Here are the guidelines:

Take larger ears, for example. When rounded, they show a strong nature that is concerned about truth and ideals, and also ambitions. If the ears are excessively large and fleshy, they point to a proud and pretentious nature.

Small ears belong to careful and prudent people who have the gift of willpower and perseverance. They also are evidence of a constantly wakeful intelligence.

As to oval ears, when they are well formed, they show wisdom. A person with oval ears loves to study and has a desire for perfection. Ears that are cauliflower-shaped and not well formed are the hallmark of frustrated, vulgar people without ideas and without charm (present company excluded).

Furthermore, the difference between a person's two ears may be of significance. If the right ear is larger than the left, the person acts in instinctive ways; in him fantasy has a stronger influence than reason. If the left ear is the larger, the person is a cerebral type who never decides things casually.

So, there you have it. Believe it (not) or not. For the rest of this article we will make an intense examination of our own ears. However, I think we should be a lot more interested in their function than in their shape. I believe we can all agree on the importance of the role that our ears play when used for their principal functions of hearing and listening. Unfortunately, the art of listening is often taken for granted until disaster strikes.

In these days of fast foods and instant texting we rarely take the time to sit and really listen to the concerns of those whose friendships we cherish. Many times, while we may be audibly hearing someone, we may not be listening with the ear of the heart. For it is with the heart's ear that we can truly hear the appeals of others.

As we listen with focused effort we will hear the needs of our neighbor. We can posture to respond to their concerns because we have been intentional in listening and identifying needs. As we listen we don't allow other distractions to enter our minds. We acknowledge our neighbor as we maintain eye contact and ask questions as he/she shares. Yes, intentional listening takes time. Intentional listening also requires a personal investment but the pay off is invaluable. We will be delighted in realizing that we can help others and make a difference in their lives. And of course, we can all learn to be better listeners and in doing so improve how we manage our individual lives. How many past mistakes would have been avoided if we had simply listened better?

Yes, sometimes we can even hear the voice of God through the needs of a neighbor. For those that are spiritually inclined, using our ears to hear the still, small voice of God's spirit can fill us with eager anticipation. Developing the ability to hear God with the ear of the soul should be a longing of all those who claim to know God and seek a stronger relationship with The Almighty. Ultimately, discerning God's voice is a deeply personal experience and comes from an intimate relationship as we hear and act on the Word of God. We may even hear God's voice through the needs of those around us.

⦁ *For I am the Lord, I do not change*
*(Micah 3:6)*

## EXPERIENCING GOD

MOE AND JOE were a couple of cheap counterfeiters. By "cheap" I mean that they were not very good at what they did. One day they accidentally printed a batch of fifteen-dollar bills. Moe asked Joe: "Man, what we gonna do with all these fifteen-dollar bills?" Joe thought for a minute and came up with a brilliant idea. "I got it," said Joe. "We'll drive up to hillbilly country and pawn-off these bills to the storekeepers." Hours later they pulled up to a dilapidated store on the side of a mountain. Moe and Joe winked at each other. They found the storeowner seated by a pot-bellied stove. Moe went up to the man and very confidently asked him, "Hey mister, can you make change for a fifteen-dollar bill?" Without batting an eyelash, the store keeper asked him back, "how do you want it son...five threes or a seven and an eight?"

The story of Moe and Joe is fiction, but this is a fact: As of 9 November 2003, the FBI had already reported the arrest of 9 people who had brazenly attempted to counterfeit the new and improved twenty-dollar bill. Other arrests have followed since that date. The new bill's decorative colors and subtle watermarks presented enough of a challenge to the alleged counterfeiters so that their cheap counterfeit reproductions were relatively easy to detect. I guess counterfeiters will always be among us.

All of this leads me to ask the following questions: Do we practice an external form of religion that hides an inner emptiness in our souls? If we do, we may be counterfeiting. The opposite conditions may also apply. For instance, do we claim to possess deep faith convictions but practice lifestyles that betray and sometimes violate the moral and ethical tenets of our faith? If we do, we may qualify as counterfeits. Do we handle our finances and resources in ways that betray our personal commitment to family, church and others? These are not merely rhetorical questions. I believe that these are questions that any rational, responsible person will need to address at some point in life's journey. I also believe that one's ability to avoid personal ambivalence is directly related to one's view of God. Let me illustrate:

A little boy offered a simple prayer: "God, please bless mom and dad, my brother and sister; and God do take care of yourself because if anything happens to you... we're all sunk!" Indeed! It gives me great comfort to know that nothing can happen to God (Amen!). It is good to know that in this fast-paced, ever-changing world of distractions, temptations, disappointments and loss that there is a constant factor (a living being) that doesn't change. There is comfort in consistency! My belief in an unchanging God also assures me of God's unchanging love for me and for all of us. I am invited to share in a relationship with this living God through the merits of Jesus Christ. This becomes the acid test for determining the sincerity of my "religion." That is, do I live with an abiding awareness of God's presence in my life? To be sure, this determines the difference between theology and religion; for while theology is thinking and talking about God, true religion/spirituality is individually experiencing God in a personal and relational way.

If I have truly encountered the reality of God, then my approach to life and the way I live it should make a difference. I will realize that any attempt at "counterfeiting" my life, ethically, morally, emotionally, or spiritually is an attempt to steal from God. This is the acid test for determining my standard of personal responsibility. In fact, I believe that my long-term potential for personal growth is directly linked to my relationship with God. Relating to God is all-encompassing and a sure formula for avoiding life's "counterfeits."

> ⚜ *God is spirit and his worshipers must worship in spirit and in truth.*
>
> *(John 4:24)*

## THE COLOR OF GOD

"WHAT COLOR IS God?" That was the question that a six-year-old African-American boy named James McBride asked his Jewish mother. James was the offspring of an interracial marriage. As he became more aware of the important things of life, his thoughts had turned to God. So, as is natural of children his age he started asking questions, which brings us to the query: "What color is God?" In his autobiographical account (*The Color of Water*, Riverhead Books 1996) Mr. McBride relates that the question came up one day as he and his mother walked home from church. The young McBride wanted to know whether God was black or white. A very wise mother answered the question in the following fashion: "Honey, God is not black. God is not white." Smiling, she continued, "God is the color of water. Water doesn't have color, and everybody can drink it, regardless of color."

That was a wise response! The answer did not miss a beat and it came from the mind and lips of one who had captured a teaching/learning moment with her child. Those moments with our children represent great opportunities to pass along eternal values and truths that will plant seeds of understanding for living healthy lives.

The six-year-old was responding to a natural instinct in the human being. He had a need to know. The child was also prepared to start perceiving God through the prism or lens of culture, race or tradition. His mother had set the matter straight by heading off any misconception. She pointed out the timeless truth that God cannot be placed in a cultural "box." She wanted her son to understand that if we are to worship and come to know God, it must be unhindered by personal prejudice or cultural stereotype. We must be careful not to categorize God through our own misconceived expectations. God is so much greater than our own, small misconceptions. You see, God's reality transcends our personal agendas.

What color is your God? What language does my God speak? What ethnicity/culture does our God prefer? Through the experience of a James McBride or a Martin Luther King Jr. we are challenged to examine our view of The Almighty and shatter all pre-conceived personal notions of God's eternal character. The sobering reality is that God is for everyone! God speaks everyone's language and invites every soul to a personal sense of relationship.

It is recorded that nearly two thousand years ago a certain woman from Samaria (present day Palestine) approached a young Jewish Rabbi. She too needed answers. She had a need to know the "color of God." She had felt a sense of awkwardness in worshiping and knowing the person of God because she wasn't quite sure whether her God had a "cultural/ethnic" preference. The young Rabbi had the opportunity to set the matter straight in her mind and in our minds.

The Rabbi's insight was compelling in its simplicity. It cut through all cultural, ethnic and racial stereotypes as he addressed the very core of the matter. The teacher explained that if we are to know and worship God we must do so unhindered by any form of personal prejudice. He was way ahead of his times in affirming basic civil rights, but his approach and focus was spiritual and always pointed towards issues of ultimate importance. Here's how he answered the woman of Samaria: "God is spirit, and those who worship must worship in spirit and truth." In other words, God is spirit, that is, no color (color of water), no material body and no cultural/ethnic preference. "Spirit and truth" are the overriding realities.

Well, let's do this. Close your eyes. Look into your soul and ask: What color is my soul? What culture is it? What language does it speak? Now, open your eyes. Friends, the family of God is a homogenous race. What this means is that after all has been said and done and this journey of life is complete neither race, nor language nor culture will be the final arbiter because God is for everyone who know and worship The Almighty in sprit and truth!

✝ *We love because he first loved us.*
*(1 John 4:19)*

## SO... WHAT'S THE QUESTION? (ON GOD'S LOVE)

THE DECADE OF the 1960's is a benchmark in the history of 20th century America. Among several significant events, the decade marked the beginning of an era of cynicism, doubt and suspicion. People started to openly question the trustworthiness of their leaders. A good number of folks had some valid reasons for doing so. Many started to question the ability of government to solve the mounting and complex problems of society. The hippies of the '60's epitomized the era's spirit of skepticism. However, in their random and carefree lifestyle, many lacked the proper answers because they failed to ask the right questions.

So, it was during one Christmas season in the '60's that in the state of Georgia, where religion was as common as fried chicken that you might often spot hand-painted signs along the highways that would read: "THE END IS COMING SOON. ARE YOU READY?" or "THE WAGES OF SIN IS DEATH." However, the disbelief and doubt of the 1960's had already permeated the hollowed highways of the Bible Belt. Under one such sign that read, "GOD IS THE ANSWER" someone had spray-painted "SO WHAT'S THE QUESTION?"

The question's cynical intent strikes at the heart of my beliefs and perhaps yours. Indeed, what is the question? Some of that skepticism may continue to persist in our hearts. Some of life's circumstances may still beg the question. You see, in moments of personal discouragement I have asked myself the "question of questions." That is, what is the question that God provides the answer to? Am I living my faith out of habit or does my faith in God provides the answer to some deep-seated, fundamental and ultimate questions that demand an answer.

Most of my own doubts circle around two questions: Do I matter and does God really care? These are the challenging questions of my faith. If God is the answer, then surely God must somehow speak to those two questions. To be sure, the problems of many lonely and discouraged people would be solved if these questions could be answered. If you and I claim to believe in God, we must be prepared to provide the answers. Can one person on a speck of a planet in this tremendous universe make a difference to the Almighty? Do I matter and does God really care? If I cannot have these two questions answered, then life becomes pretty meaningless for me.

Placed neatly in the prophetic pages of the Bible, in the ancient book of Isaiah, we can start addressing these two questions. Written some seven hundred years before the birth of Christ, we find the people of Israel dealing with precisely those questions: *Do I matter and does God really care?* The questions are answered with an affirmation so simple in its clarity and ever so clear in its application:

> *Do you not know? Have you not heard? The Lord is the everlasting God, the Creator of the ends of the earth. He will not grow tired or weary and his understanding no one can fathom. He gives strength to the weary and increases the power of the weak. Even youths grow tired and weary and young men stumble and fall; but those who hope in the Lord will renew their strength. They will soar on wings like*

*eagles; they will run and not grow weary, they will
walk and not be faint. (Isaiah 40:28-31)*

If God cares enough to provide me with this kind of hope, then I do matter, and God does care. But, if God does care then why is there so much suffering in the world? Again, the answer to this question may appear simple, because it is. The answer is: Because God loves us! Say what?!... Yes, because God so loves us we possess freedom to choose. We are given the freedom to love God back and to hope in the Almighty's providential care. Much suffering is due to the bad choices that we make. Much suffering can be avoided and even eliminated by exercising our freedom to have fellowship with God.

Hope in the Lord ... and renew your strength!

⊹ *You gave me life and showed me kindness, and in
your providence watched over my spirit.*
*(Job 10:12)*

## A WHALE OF A STORY (ON GOD'S PROVIDENCE)

I GUESS IT was a day like any other day for Chippy the parakeet. He was a happy parakeet, although his wings had been clipped. Chippy was a happy parakeet because he was a singing parakeet. One morning his owner let him out of his cage and, as customary, Chippy was singing. But, the event that was about to befall him was beyond anything he could have imagined. You see, four-year old Jonathan was on the loose. Jonathan was the family terrorist, able to create madness and confusion at a moment's notice.

12

Jonathan noticed that his mother's vacuum cleaner was at his grasp and he just loved the noise it made and what it did. So, he decided to experiment on Chippy. He turned the vacuum on, took the vacuum's nozzle and put it up to Chippy. What followed was a horrifying moment both for Chippy and Jonathan's mother, who walked in on Jonathan at the very moment that Chippy got sucked in.

She rushed over to the machine, disassembled it as fast as she could and carefully and gently removed Chippy from the vacuum cleaner bag. For the parakeet the whole event must have felt like a lifetime. Yes, Chippy was still alive but he had a dazed look, the "500-yard stare." And, oh by the way, Chippy doesn't sing anymore he just sits and stares. Chippy had a rough day. The moral of the story: "Stuff happens."

I don't know about you, but when stuff happens to me I need to believe in a God that will intervene unexpectedly. I also need to believe that my God will act purposely and redemptively. Such was the experience of an ancient biblical prophet named Jonah. Jonah is popularly known as the prophet who was swallowed up by a "great fish." It is a fascinating biblical epic depicting the life of a man who suddenly, unexpectedly found himself in the "belly of the beast." To be sure, Jonathan needed some immediate, purposeful and divine intervention. You can read Jonah's account in the biblical book of the same name.

As for the "great fish" or the "sea monster" which swallowed Jonah, the question has come up: was this a real fish? Was it a whale, a shark, a mutated fish or the Lockness monster? And... here's the answer: I don't know, and I don't care because that's not the point. If we focus just on these types of questions we will miss the point of the biblical message. So, what is the point? What is the statement? The statement is: My God is great enough! My God is great enough to act purposely, redemptively and decisively even in the midst of my darkest moments.

> ⊹ *In my distress I called to the Lord, and he answered*
> *me. From the depths of the grave I called for help,*
> *and you listened to my cry.*
>
> *(Jonah 2:1-2)*

Is that the kind of God you believe in? And… that's the point. My God is great enough! Now then, since we've settled that… let's move on. An awesome God acts in unexpected ways at unexpected times. Therefore, let us not try to out-think nor second-guess God.

> ⊹ *For my thoughts are not your thoughts, neither are*
> *your ways my ways, declares the Lord.*
> *(Isaiah 55:8)*

An awesome God acts with purpose. Now, we may not understand the purpose but whenever we are at the end of our rope and our backs are up against the wall, we can become hopeless, desperate and visionless. In those moments belief in the God who is great enough will make all the difference.

Remember Chippy? He had been saved by the hand of his master, but the poor little guy could not see the big picture. God spares us that we may see the big picture and sing a new song.

> ⊹ *For in him we live and move and have our being.*
> *(Acts 17:28)*

## Courage to Believe

If we are to believe current data, there will be anywhere from 60-80 million people in America's Christian churches this coming Sunday. If we add to this figure the number of those attending temples and mosques of other religions, we may start to believe that America is a religious country. Indeed, all these people represent a cross section of the population. They come from all walks of life, ethnicities and levels of earning. Many occupy positions of leadership in businesses, government, and the military. As for the ones that are not in attendance, I assure you, they too ultimately believe in something or someone (even if they just believe in themselves as the ultimate authority). All of them are representative of a people living in times of tremendous need for continuous integrity and courage.

Attempts have been made to define the word "courage." Ernest Hemingway simply defined it as follows: "courage is grace under pressure." I like this definition, but I have a preference for the definition offered by the Reverend Gardner Taylor (1918-2015) of the Concord Church of Christ in Brooklyn, New York: "Courage is reason turned to faith in God." Both definitions imply action but more importantly, both definitions denote that courage is a quality of the human spirit. Although often described in terms of acts or actions, courage goes beyond the physical expression of doing something. Courage is an inner attribute of the spirit that one either possesses or not. It must rest based on a strong moral and spiritual foundation. I believe this is so because I maintain that courage is a quality that resides in the very being of God. I will go a step further and assert that the Almighty wants us to possess courage.

We will be looking at the topic of courage through the eyes of a battle-hardened veteran of many campaigns. His name was Joshua and he was the military commander for the people of Israel during Moses' lifetime. After the death of Moses, Joshua became his successor. Joshua's experience stands out as one of the great biblical narratives that address the topic of courage. As his story unfolds, Joshua's spirit is impressed with a command from God to be courageous.

I find it interesting that Joshua, a battle-hardened veteran and commander of Israel's warriors, would have to be commanded to be courageous. To be sure, his life's experiences had already demonstrated that he was a man of courage. Yet, in his heart Joshua felt compelled by God to be courageous. Why? Well, I believe that he was afraid. Joshua was scared and discouraged at that juncture in his life. He feared the uncharted waters that lay before him.

Friends, I want to address the topic of courage because from time-to-time I (and perhaps you) become fearful. This happens especially when I am relying just on myself. It also happens when I acknowledge that I have reached the limits of my personal abilities (and we all have those limitations). You see, sooner or later we will all know the hard places in life. Sooner or later we will all know the lonely places in life. Sooner or later we will all have to believe in something or someone. It is at those moments that we can choose to believe that God is always with us. Therefore, we can take courage. Those are the moments when courage goes beyond action and must be defined in terms of the inner core of one's spirit.

Whenever faced with the inner demons of fear and feelings of personal inadequacies, we need to know that the courage to live and rise above the elements flows from God. I submit that if our courage to live does not flow from God, we will become arrogant and in time, unhappy.

Courage is making a choice that we will not be victimized by life. While we may have no control over the many circumstances of life, we do have a measure of control in how we choose to respond. In those moments we can decide that our lives can be an instrument in the hands of God. To be a successful veteran of many of life's campaigns one must appropriate courage, God's courage, because there are places yet to go where we have not set foot. There may be some big battles awaiting us. But remember, the promise of the Almighty is: "God will be with you wherever you go" (Joshua 1:9b). It is a great promise, a great truth and a great reality for those that have the courage to embrace it with all their hearts.

⁘ *'What is truth?' Pilate asked.*

*(John 18:38)*

## Don't be Fooled...Catch the Light!

On April Fools Day people attempt to dupe others into thinking that what is true is not or vice versa. I believe that people fall for these pranks because there is an innate drive in human beings to know and believe in the truth. When formulating the theory of relativity Albert Einstein was attempting to dispel some myths and half-truths to arrive at the facts. What he offered to mankind was a gift of intuitive insight and knowledge that revolutionized the modern era. Dr. Einstein once said that the reason that he could formulate the theory of relativity was because there is one thing in the physical, material universe that is unchangeable. That one immutable factor is the speed of light. It is one of the only known constants in the physical universe.

Light travels at 186,000 miles per second. That means that any glimmer of light will travel seven (7) times around the world in one second flat. That is an amazing thing! The power of light is piercing. You just know when there is just the slightest glimmer of light in a room. You cannot deny when light has pierced the darkness. In fact, darkness and light cannot coexist together at the same time and in the same place.

I'll even go further than this. Without light we would not exist (and I'm not fooling). Light gives warmth. The sun's light nourishes our very being. Without light it would be a world of total darkness. It would be a freezing, lifeless uninhabitable planet floating in the galaxy. So…let there be light!

From time immemorial light has been a symbol for the good and true. Better yet, it has also become a symbol pointing toward that, which is ultimately good. That which is ultimately good must be unchangeable. It must pierce the heart as light pierces the darkness and it must be consistent from generation to generation. The radiance of what is good and true cannot be denied. When we are exposed to this "light" it will uncover the presence of any "darkness" in our life and will challenge us to dispel that which is not good and true. We then become responsible for the truth. We also assume responsibility for living and projecting the truth.

The Light of Truth is Functional. Just as a lighthouse projects light at all hours of the night, we are always called to shed light. This requires an intentional and self-conscious awareness of our own need for goodness and truth. It will require a level of personal preparedness in shedding light (truth) whenever necessary. C.S. Lewis expressed it well in his book, Miracles: "We believe that the sun is in the sky at mid-day.* Not because we can so clearly see the sun,

---

\*     *Miracles*, Harper Collins, New York, copyright 1947, 1960, 1974,1996

but because we can see everything else!" What is good and true is like that. It helps us to see clearly everything else.

The Light of Truth is Practical. That which is true will show the direction to go. It will give security to the voyager and shows the way to safety. There is something interesting about the truth. Once you are there it surrounds you with its sense of security.

The Light of Truth is Praiseworthy. It saves lives. Like a city on a mountaintop whose light cannot be denied, truth is the very extension of God's refulgence lighting the way for us.

A slightly drunk man is seen crawling on his hands and knees under a streetlight. He's looking for something. A friend sees him and asks what he's looking for. "I'm looking for my house keys," the man answers. Wanting to help him, the friend says, "Give me an idea where you think you dropped the keys." "Over there in the bushes," said the man. "Then why in the world are you looking over here?!" his friend cried out in disbelief. "Because this is where the light is." Modern man can sometimes be best depicted in that most revealing encounter. That is, knowing that we have lost something and equally knowing that the light (truth) is the answer!

> ✤ *Then you will know the truth, and the truth will*
> *set you free.*
>
> (John 8:32)

## STICKING TO THE TRUTH

IT WAS A nice Sunday morning after church. The two brothers were playing separately in the back yard. Suddenly, the boys noticed a wild thrashing in the bushes. It got their attention. Out of the bushes emerged "Mate," their Labrador Retriever. The dog was ferociously shaking a black and white rabbit. They immediately realized that the rabbit belonged to Mrs. Clausen, the widow next door. Mate, of course, was oblivious to that fact.

Well, there was nothing else they could do but tell their father. They had confidence that "dad" would fix the problem. Past experience had taught the boys that their old man never despaired and never acknowledged failure. So, the boys took the rabbit-problem to dad. The father studied the situation and told the boys not to worry. He said: "Look! Just hose-off the little fella real good so he looks nice and clean. Brush him down with this towel and stick him back in the cage. Mrs. Clausen is still at church. When she comes home and discovers her rabbit she'll be a little upset but she'll figure that he just died a natural death…. Oh, by the way, be sure and tie-up the dog."

The boys did exactly as instructed and then hid in the bushes to observe the widow when she noticed the rabbit. Sure enough, when Mrs. Clausen arrived and saw the rabbit in the cage she let out the worst scream imaginable. She hollered, shrieked, cried and yelled. She asked God all kinds of questions. The boys, accompanied by their mom and dad, ran over and commenced to comfort and calm her down. They finally got her to calm down enough and asked her to explain what had happened. In between sniffs and sobs she finally got it out: "I buried that rabbit three days ago!"

I've shared all that to state this:

- If you want to know the truth you have to dig it up for yourself (the dog knew the truth but he couldn't share it).

- If truth comes to you second-hand, you may not be able to defend it or believe it (the boys didn't know the "entire" truth).

20

- The source of your truth is as important as the truth itself.

- You cannot create your own truth. Truth is truth.

For the person of faith, the source, the origin and the consistency of truth is of uncontestable importance. Indeed, the Scriptures make the bold assertion "then you will know the truth, and the truth will set you free" (The Holy Bible, John 8:32).

A philosophy professor always started each new semester by asking his class: "Do you believe that it can be proven that there are absolute values such as truth?" To be sure, there were always a number of students who argued that truth is relative. That is, that there is no single truth that can be applied universally. The professor would then proceed to prove his point: "Regardless of what you think I want you to know that absolute truth can be demonstrated and if you don't accept what I say… I'll flunk you!" One angry student would habitually respond: "That's not fair." "You have just proven my point," the professor would respond. "You've just appealed to a higher authority of fairness… THE TRUTH!"

Let's face it. Truth can be a scary thing. Coming face to face with the truth will challenge us to change for the better, and changing bad habits is not an easy thing. Truth may even demand a radical change of direction on our part. Facing the truth and acknowledging its claim on our lives is as much an act of courage as it is an act of faith. Submitting to the truthful claims of God translates into the best possible use of our rational powers. Indeed, the truth will set us free to live right, "to act justly and to love mercy and to walk humbly with your God" (Micah 6:8)

⊹ *...faith without deeds is dead.*

*(James 2:26b)*

## WALK THE TALK (THE ETHICS OF IT ALL)

SOME YEARS AGO, it was reported that a major railway was looking for a way to test the windshields of their locomotives. They heard that an airline company had designed an unusual test cannon for precisely this purpose. The airline company used the cannon to fire lifeless chickens at great force into the windshields of passenger jets. They did this to make sure that the designs and the materials were up to par.

The railway company had no problem in borrowing the equipment. They bought some dead chickens at the local supermarket and the cannon was loaded, aimed and fired at the locomotive's windshield. The bird smashed through the windshield, broke the engineer's chair and made a large dent in the rear wall. An investigation ensued. An expert went to work on the problem and quickly concluded. "No problem," the investigator said, "the next time you use a chicken, just make sure it isn't frozen!"

The truth is like that it isn't it! It smashes through layers of misperceptions. It smashes through a heart made hard by years of disillusionments, years of being lied to and years of being hurt.

When heard and acted upon, the truth smashes through the impurities of our lives and shakes the very foundation of our character (or lack thereof). The truth will smash the spiritual confusion in our lives and will restructure us in ways that we could not imagine.

I believe that we live in an age that is hungering for the truth. We're seeing a generation of people that are seeking answers to serious questions. A generation that has broken barriers in a number of areas, affecting many facets of society. To be sure, the era of internet technology has opened us to an avalanche of information that has created a super market of ideas, opinions and options. In that data milieu people seek answers to questions that may reveal ultimate reality.

So, are there transcendent truths that cut across all belief systems and cultures and ages? I believe that there are. The longer I study the great religions of the world, the more I realize that each celebrates and refines concepts that reflect the same elemental truths. It is interesting to identify that the fundamental message conveyed to the faithful of different traditions is not new and unique but ancient and applicable throughout the ages. For instance, the Golden Rule is one of the most universal truth for ethical behavior held in common by virtually every philosophical and religious system:

> *"Treat others as you would like them to treat you."*
> *(Jesus of Nazareth)*

> *"Do not do to others all that which is not well for oneself." (Zoroaster)*

> *"Hurt not others with that which hurts you."*
> *(Buddha)*

> *"Do not do to others what you do not want others to do to you." (Confucius)*

> *"May I do to others as I would that they should do to me." (Plato)*

*"Do not do to others what, if it were done to you, would cause you pain." (Mahabharata, Hindu)*

*"Do not do to others what you would not have them do to you." (Rabbi Hillel)*

*"None of you truly have the faith if you do not desire for your brother that which you desire for yourself." (Muhammad)*

*"Lay not on an soul a load which you would not wish to be laid on you and desire not for anyone the things you would not desire for yourself." (Baha'u'llah, Bahai)*

This is not to say that all religions are the same. Indeed, each of the world's faiths must be understood and respected within its own context. However, it is important to identify those points of convergence where these different streams of thought meet.

The Golden Rule is just one example of a number of truisms that when loaded into the cannon, aimed and fired away will simplify life and create positive, long-lasting effects.

# SECTION II
## FAITH'S JOURNEY

 *...and you will be my people, and I will be your God.*

*(Jeremiah 11:4b)*

## AN OATH OF LOYALTY

NOT VERY FAR from Jerusalem, you will find the abandoned ruins of Masada. After the fall of Jerusalem in 70 A.D., the last Jewish holdouts retreated to this mountaintop citadel. Masada had become a bastion of defiance against Rome's stranglehold over the land. Flavius Silva, the Roman General pursued these last defenders of the Jewish revolt. The General laid siege and had his troops construct a ramp that lead up to the fortress' ramparts. In fact, the remains of the ramp and portions of the Roman army's encampment have been excavated and are still visible today.

When the ramp was finally completed, the Roman soldiers invaded Masada. To their amazement, the Romans discovered that a mass suicide had taken place! All the inhabitants of the fortress, men, women and children, were found dead. They had decided to take their own lives rather that succumb at the hands of their enemies.

Today, recruits in the Israeli armed forces are taught what happened at Masada. When they are sworn in as soldiers they are actually taken to the ruins of Masada. As part of their ceremony the recruits are asked to repeat the phrase, "Masada will never fall again." It has become a ritual which is repeated again and again for each group of recruits. Indeed, Masada is burned into the consciousness of a nation through remembrances. "Masada will never fall again" is a symbol of a nation's resolution. It is an oath of loyalty recommitting faithful soldiers to "remember the past in order to live for a brighter future."

"I pledge allegiance to the flag of the United States of America and to the republic for which it stands. One nation under God...." "Oh say can you see by the dawn's early light what so proudly we hailed at the twilight's last gleaming...." Perhaps there is that family heirloom passed down from one generation to another. Could there be a wedding band worn as a visible reminder "to love and to cherish until death us do part?" We may wear a cross or some other symbol of our faith. Maybe a simple commemorative meal can help us to honor an event or cherish the memory of a person we love. All of these are powerful symbols that will help us to remember the past in order to live for a brighter future.

In the midst of these different experiences we can well-up with emotions and tear-filled eyes. To be sure, these powerful national and personal symbols can recommit us to our deepest convictions and longings. All of us need these viable symbols that help us to remember the past in order to live for a brighter future. In his book The Lord is my Shepherd (Knopf, New York 2003) Rabbi Harold S. Kushner brings it into focus with the following observation: "He (God) has given us memory that we might learn the lessons of the past." Indeed, the past can be filled with invaluable lessons that we can remember either in celebration for the great times or guarded awareness for past mistakes lest those mistakes be repeated.

In my faith tradition I am often reminded of the important role played by promises, oaths and the symbols that point to their efficacy. "Yeah, though I walk through the valley of the shadow of death, I will fear no evil for thou art with me." (Psalm 23:4)

"I will never leave you nor forsake you." (Joshua 1:5)

"I will not leave you comfortless." (Gospel of John 14:18)

"In my Father's house are many rooms... I am going there to prepare a place for you...." (Gospel of John 14:2-3)

As I am reminded of God's oaths of loyalty to me I become involved in a type of prophetic activity. I remember the past promises, reaffirm their present reality and set my eyes on a brighter future. If I do so faithfully, I can discover the two greatest adventures of the purpose-filled life: discovering God's will and obeying God's will.

As I remember the past I will live presently for a brighter future because if the future belongs to God (and it does) then my future can only be as bright as God's light.

⊕ *So I say, live by the Spirit, and you will not gratify the desires of the sinful nature.*

*(Galatians 5:16)*

## ARE YOU DANCING ALONE?

A PARTICULARLY VICIOUS rumor has been circulating for years. The rumor is this: "Baptists don't dance." How absurd! My friends, today I take pen in hand in order to dispel this terrible rumor. I aim to set the record straight. I am here to tell you that this is not true. It is an error of errors and here is the truth. It is not that Baptists don't dance. The truth is that Baptists can't dance! I guess that if we Baptists could dance we would… but we can't. I speak from personal experience.

Well, that is not the main purpose behind this article. There is a much more important reason. My rationale for writing is somewhat related to dancing. You see, there are times in life that we may feel like we are dancing alone. That is, dancing without a partner. Oh, you can just imagine the awkwardness of dancing alone. You know, the feet are moving but there's no accompanying partner (whether you are leading or following). In dancing alone there is this strange, awkward sense of isolation. There is a strange feeling of being alone because … you are alone.

Consider this other consideration. There are times in life that we may be dancing with a partner but find ourselves seriously out of step. Not only is it awkward but it can be absolutely embarrassing. The potential for stepping on your partner's toes while being out of step can make for stressful and anxious moments.

I believe that if we follow this analogy we will discover a spiritual truth for application. You see, there have been moments in my life that I have felt like I was dancing alone. I have felt that God was not there. Perhaps I may have fallen seriously out of step with God's direction for my life. Those have been anxious and even scary moments in my life.

Indeed, there are a number of things that can go wrong when "dancing alone" or being out of step with the things of God. A sense of reckless abandonment can tend to influence us when "dancing alone." Perhaps jealousy, hatred, discord, selfish ambition or even envy can encroach on our relative stability. This short list can remind us of those moments when we have flirted with the abyss.

When being out of step with the things of God thoughts may have crossed our minds that have shocked us. It is precisely at those moments that we are to be ever on our guard, like sentinels, being aware of the emotional and spiritual struggle that is taking place.

But,… thanks be to God! There is a choice each day. As children of God we can make a choice. We can choose to be "in step" with the things of God. It is great to be free. It is double great to be free to do what is right. When we make this choice we will be in step with the Spirit of God. Interesting and good things then start to happen. In time, our efforts will give good fruit. You see, as a tree grows and develops it will give fruit in its season. Inner peace, patience, instinctive kindness, faithfulness and self-control are just some of the fruits of a good life when we get in step with God's direction. When we are in step a sense of growing harmony can pervade our work environment and our home.

How would we rate ourselves when it comes to walking in step with the Spirit of God? Are we dancing alone? Are we making questionable decisions that are later bringing negative repercussions? Are we making decisions outside of the wise council of the Almighty? Are we following our own lead by allowing our own stubborn pride and arrogance to get in the way of wisdom? Are we seeking the advice of those that live with an abiding knowledge of the goodness of God?

Friends, we don't need to be dancing alone and we don't need to be out of step. Each and every day we can make the right choice and make the music of the soul.

⊹ *God also testified to it by signs, wonders and various miracles….*

*(Hebrews 2:4)*

## CATCHING ELECTRICITY (ON MIRACLES)

SOME YEARS AGO a major electrical company received a letter from a third grade girl asking for information for her class project. The letter read something like this:

> *"Dear Sirs:*
>
> *I'm trying to get all the information I can, so please send me any booklets and papers you have. Also, would it be asking too much for you to send me a little sample of electricity?"*

You and I may smile at the innocence expressed in this child's request. This little girl was asking for a miracle of sorts. However, we are sometimes like this child. There are moments that we deeply desire a miracle of sorts. There are times that we need to capture or recapture a jolt of electricity to restart our lives. We may even clamor for a miracle.

Think about it. How many times have we wanted concrete examples of the great mysteries of God? How many times have we asked for a miracle (however small) as tangible proof of God's presence, concern and love?

Each year, as we prepare to celebrate the Easter and Passover seasons, two major religions of the world will commemorate events in their histories which were, to say the least, miraculous. The historical claims of Christians and Jews point us to a time in which the presence, concern and love of God were manifested in extraordinary ways.

So, while the Easter season may signal to many people the onset of Spring and the Summer months that follow, I affirm that the resurrection of Jesus Christ, as recorded in the Scriptures, stand for a lot more. If approached with the proper spirit, an open heart and the eyes of faith this "miracle of Easter" may even give you a jolt, a jump-start because it will remind you that miracles of personal renewal can still be manifested in our lives. Miracles remind us that the Almighty continues to express love and concern through his divine presence.

Now, I know that it is not cool to believe in miracles these days. I know that in some circles it may not be the politically correct thing to believe. It may even be perceived as infantile that a grown man or woman would believe in the "M" word. Nevertheless, I will go as far as stating that I believe that belief in the miraculous is the meeting place between the transcendent (God) and the creation (us), with faith acting as the bridge.

The problem we may have with the miraculous may lie in our personal expectations. We may expect that a miracle must be a stupendous, spectacular and bigger-than-life event. While it can be that, I believe that for the most part miraculous events occur on a smaller, down-to-earth scale as seen through the eyes of faith.

Here is my experience with miracles (don't worry; I'm not going to shock you). A miracle can stop you from drinking the bitter waters of life. A miracle can replace the "old wine" of hopelessness with the "new wine" of personal renewal and hope. The miraculous assumes that the following exists:

1. A sense of personal relationship with God.
2. A sense of personal need for God's presence, concern and love.
3. A personal petition for God's provision according to God's plan and purpose.

Ultimately, a miracle is seen and experienced through the eyes of faith and as seen through those eyes we may just catch a little sample of (God's) electricity.

⊹ ..."Listen to me, Judah and people of Jerusalem! Have faith in the LORD your God and you will be upheld....

*(2 Chronicles 20:20)*

## IT'S WHAT'S INSIDE THAT COUNTS!

WITH ANDY'S FIFTH birthday coming up and with Disney's Pocahontas animated film on the verge of being released that day, you know where he wanted to go. So, mom and dad agreed where to take him on that afternoon. Getting ready to go, mom instructed: "Andy, go get my purse then go to the refrigerator, pick a snack and put it inside to have at the movies." Mom assumed that Andy would pick a granola bar or perhaps some cookies. They arrived at the movie theatre and had been there for a full thirty minutes when Andy leaned over and said: "Mom…can I have my ice cream sandwich now?" The moral of the story: "it's what's inside that counts."

Do you worship God? Do I delight in the worship of The Almighty? Do we understand what it means to exalt God with the fullness (the inside) of all we are? To be sure these are not the kind of questions that we encounter on a regular basis. Yet, these are the very questions that any believer in the living God must answer as part of a reality check. Indeed, the worship of God in all of its fullness is fundamental to our design and purpose. It is one of the great privileges of the faith-filled life. Here's what I mean:

✢ "Praise the Lord, O my soul; all my inmost being,
   praise his holy name.
   Praise the Lord, O my soul, who forgives all your sins
   And heals all your deceases, who redeems your life
   from the pit
   And crowns you with love and compassion, who sat-
   isfies your desires with
   Good things, so that your youth is renewed like the
   eagles."

(Psalm 103:1-5)

You see, when it comes to the worship of God "it's what's inside that counts" and there is no faking it. Personal worship is either real or it is a hollow moment. King David of Israel was an older man when he penned the words found in the Psalm. The Psalm is filled with exuberance and praise. His desire was to remind all who read the words that there are many reasons to worship God with the fullness of our spirit. In other words, if we would find out what is inside our lives and praise God with the "insideness" of our souls then we will begin to capture the essence of worship and the great privilege we are afforded when we worship God.

The 103rd Psalm is like that. It is so filled with praise that it is impossible to contain. The Psalm reminds us of what God has done. It reminds us of the greatness of God. It reads like the Sears catalog of God's goodness and enumerates the wonderful privileges that faith brings. The Psalm uses action words to remind us that God forgives, rescues, heals and rejuvenates our spirits. It reminds us that God embraces and envelopes our whole life. If this is true, and it is, then all that is within me should seek to praise God in a spirit of gratitude. In our iniquities we praise God for His mercy. In our families, we praise God for the blessings of family. Indeed it is a great privilege of faith to experience the worship of the living God. In short, don't forget the benefits from God.

I remember years ago The American Express Company crafted the motto "Membership has its Privileges." The motto was carefully formulated. Its words were skillfully selected to project an air of importance and elitism. Many people were willing to pay the membership fee to experience the privileges that came with it. In stark contrast, the gift of faith avails mankind the two most important privileges this side of heaven: The knowledge of God and the worship of God (and by the way, you don't have to pay a membership fee).

A by-product of this privilege is being crowned with love and compassion. This we need to remember because it contains endless possibilities for experiencing it in so many ways. When we worship the living God we stop to smell the roses; we take pause and celebrate God's eternal source of love, grace & compassion as we praise God in the fullness of our soul.

Don't forget what God has done! Don't forget: "it's what's inside that counts!"

> ⭑ *I am saying this for your own good, not to restrict you, but that you may live in a right way in undivided devotion to the Lord.*
> *(1 Corinthians 7:35)*

## DON'T HESITATE, DEDICATE!

SOMETIMES WE ARE like the little boy whose mother asked him to go to the cellar and get a can of tomato soup from the pantry. The little fella didn't want to go. "Mom, it's dark in there and I'm scared." "It's O.K. Johnny" she reassured him. "Go and get a can of tomato soup." "But mom, it's dark and I'm too scared to go in there by myself." "It's O.K. son... God will be in there with you. Now, you go and get that can of soup." So, the little boy went to the basement door, opened it slowly and peeked inside. It was darker than dark! He was scared. His hands trembled but he came up with an idea. He looked down the stairs into the darkness and yelled down: "God, if you're down there would you get me a can of tomato soup?"

Sometimes we are like that little boy because we may realize that trusting God can be a scary proposition. Perhaps it may dawn on us that deciding to step out on faith into seemingly dark territory and unchartered waters can scare us "hairless." As we experience the fear of the unknown we may feel restrained, immobilized and perhaps paralyzed. Fear can and will deny us of God's richest blessings if we allow it. Fear can create in us a sense of panic that will render us useless in our individual as well as collective effectiveness. We will lose our salt and flavor and our vitality. Consequently, we will lose our motivation to dedicate ourselves to those worthiest, most honorable and godly tasks.

Well, I don't know how the story ended with little Johnny and his conversation with God. But, I suspect that God may have answered back "Hey Johnny... come... we'll both get it together!"

Risking beyond our fears requires dedication. It must be a dedication borne of a vision for the future and it must also be a dedication that risks for God. Long-term consistency is typically its most noticeable characteristic.

In trying to capture a fuller understanding of what it means to dedicate I try to look for models. These models are notable people who have achieved and fleshed-out their vision for life through consistent dedication. The list of these people is exhaustive. However, there is one individual that came to my mind: King Solomon of Israel.

Nine hundred years before the birth of Christ he set out to construct a magnificent temple in Jerusalem. It took twenty years to build and it stood until 70 A.D. Today the Wailing Wall is the only physical vestige remaining of this once grand temple. Solomon's Temple was an architectural marvel. (Read about it in the Bible, in the book of First Kings.) Built on a grand scale, it was a visible, public statement of a people's dedication to risk for God and to risk with God.

The successful completion of this grand structure teaches us a few valuable lessons regarding the meaning of dedication. Indeed, if dedication is to be effective at all it must be accompanied by personal sacrifice and unselfish acts. A personal commitment to trust in the God who will uphold, and preserve is an indispensable factor as well. All throughout the process of dedication there must be an affirmation of personal accountability in seeing it through.

Friends, we cannot separate dedication from personal commitment and we cannot separate dedication from personal vision. I believe this must begin with a personal commitment to the things of God and then a commitment to serve others. Everything else flows from there. Think of the revolutionary, positive changes that would take place if we all decided to make this our guiding principle.

Let's face it, "Commitment" has become a dirty word for some and yet all of us make commitments everyday. Heaven forbid that we default on any of those commitments. Now, is God any less worthy of our devotion and dedication? Dedication (to God) is a win-win situation!

⁘ *Trust in the LORD with all your heart and lean not on your own understanding; in all your ways acknowledge him, and he will make your paths straight.*

*(Proverbs 3:5-6)*

## TOO SHORT TO YO-YO!

I REMEMBER THE time that I bought my youngest son his first yo-yo. What a day it was! At that time Danny was four years old and his reaction to the gift was pure joy. It was one of those deluxe, professional-grade models that in the right hands could perform the most unbelievable tricks imaginable. As I gave him the gift I took great delight in just watching his excitement over this new toy. But the joy only lasted about 10 seconds. You see my son Danny had made a disappointing discovery. His discovery: he was too short to yo-yo. His legs were too short, and the string was too long. His mood changed instantly. His frustration level was discernibly HIGH. Danny realized, in his own special way, that life was a little more complicated than he thought.

I suggest that being too short to yo-yo is a metaphor for the trying times in life. It is a metaphor for those hard places that we find ourselves in occasionally. When was the first time that life became complicated for you? When was the last time you noticed that your legs were too short, that your yo-yo string was too long and that your arms were too weak? When have you had that sinking feeling that comes when your dreams and /or desires were not going according to your expectations?

Indeed, in those moments of testing you become keenly aware that you are truly not in control. You may even discover that your faith starts to falter. What happens when your faith starts to crumble? Those are the hard places in life when your emotions and life's events get the better of you and you may even start to seriously doubt in yourself and even in the very God that has given you eternal assurance of His faithfulness. In those moments you will struggle with questions of importance such as "why do good things always happen to the bad guys?"

Have you been there? I have and those are scary moments in life. Are you there now? How do you cope with unfulfilled dreams? What do you do when your faith falters? It is important to remember during such uncontrollable events that there is still one component of life that you still have control over. You do have control over how you decide to respond to the difficulties and challenges of life. You can choose to exercise control over your response.

So, what do you do when your faith falters? (Or when you're too short to YO-YO)

LOOK AROUND: Your difficulties are put in perspective when you look around and see the plight of those that must contend with much graver circumstances. Your problems suddenly pale by comparison. While this doesn't diminish the importance of your problem it will hopefully help you understand that your situation is solvable and manageable by comparison. Look around and see the lives of people who have successfully surmounted their obstacles. I'm not a betting man, but 9 out of 10 you'll discover that they are persons of faith in themselves and God (most importantly).

LOOK INSIDE: I mean, really look inside you. Who are you? Do you know yourself? What do you ultimately believe in, deep inside? Sometimes we hesitate to look inside because we dare not admit that we may be the cause of our own problems. Look "inside" and have the courage to make the necessary changes towards a better person.

LOOK UP: As you look up you may discover, to your delight, that the Almighty is there. As you acknowledge your need for God His divine, invisible hand will lift your spirit. In that instant of personal encounter, the Spirit of God will bring clarity and new direction. At that moment you will find God where He does His work: in your heart.

⁂ *Now faith is being sure of what we hope for and certain of what we do not see.*

*(Hebrews 11:1)*

## Did the Unicorn Make the Cut?

THE STORY OF Noah and the Ark has not suffered from loss of popularity nor fascination over all these centuries. It is a classic epic of biblical proportions (no pun intended). It is also extremely marketable. There is a niche in the toy industry built around the manufacture and sale of the ark. Children's books and scholarly commentaries line the shelves in bookstores and libraries. In fact, political difficulties and challenging logistical problems have not stopped expeditions from climbing the icy peaks of Mt. Ararat (borders of turkey and Russian republics) in hopes of finding the petrified fossil remains of the Ark. The question has remained: "Were they looking in the right place?"

Entire theories endeavor to explain how Noah managed to deal with the dinosaurs. Other explanations tackle how Noah managed to fit all the vast varieties of animal species (male and female) into the Ark. To be sure, the search for the answer has been known to create heated debates in some circles.

I wonder, really, whether we are just burning valuable energy on the wrong questions regarding Noah and the Ark. I am of the opinion that the biblical account of Noah, his family, the Ark and the smelly animals he had to live with for 150 days is much broader and deeper than those other questions that many people are burning energy and effort over. Yes, there is ample geological evidence to support the ancient flood theory which was massive and devastating. How did Noah manage to fit all existing species of animals into a boat 450 feet long by 75 feet wide and 45 feet high and feed all of them for 150 days? I don't know. I submit that the account of Noah and the Ark was not written to settle scientific arguments. When I read this marvelous epic I'm after bigger fish. When I read this classic story, I seek to draw truth that transcends science and leads me into the realm of God's eternal and consistent principles. As far as I'm concerned debates about geology are too narrow. Debates about the logistics and size of the Ark are too myopic. The heart of the story is much larger than that.

The heart of this account is Noah's journey of faith. To our delight we will discover that there is much to learn for our own journey of faith through Noah's story. How we mature and develop our personal faith is vastly more important than polemics, debates and arguments. Our faith is what will carry me through this journey and beyond. In fact, our faith is eternal. Long after you and I are gone, debates will continue, egos will still clash but our individual faith is forever!

Anyway, what is faith? Here's a classic definition: "Faith is being sure of what we hope for and certain of what we do not see" (Holy Bible, Hebrews 11:1). If you asked Noah to define faith he might have said, "Faith is readiness to obey." Obedience is a function of responsive faith. Therefore, faith and obedience are action words. In fact, obedience demonstrates the measure of our faith in the things of God. That, in a nutshell, is the central message of Noah's journey. Indeed, the extent of Noah's obedience is publicly displayed on a mammoth scale. Love can make us do that.

When one of my children was 3 to 6 years old he had a fantastic habit, which wore off as he approached his teen years. Without warning, even in the middle of restaurants, he would yell out, "Dad,

I love you." And, I would yell it right back, "I love you too!" It was fun, and we were neither ashamed nor embarrassed.

Noah's unashamed demonstration of obedience was public and unconditional. God's demonstration of love for Noah and his family was a commitment of the Almighty's unchanging integrity, protection and power. That's where I want to be!

> ⊹ *Make every effort to live in peace with all men.*
> *(Hebrews 12:14)*

## BLESSED ARE THE PEACEMAKERS

WHO CAN FORGET the remarkable exploits of Lucy and Charlie Brown? In one classic encounter between them we find Lucy chasing Charlie Brown and shouting at the top of her voice: "I'll get you, Charlie Brown! I'll catch you and when I do I'm going to knock your block off!" Suddenly, Charlie Brown, who's somewhat of a philosopher and student of human behavior, screeches to a halt. He whirls around and says to Lucy: "wait a minute. If you and I, as relatively small children with relatively small problems can't sit down and talk through our problems in a mature way...how can we expect that nations of the world to..." POW!! Lucy slugged him. After hitting him Lucy said: "I had to hit him quick...he was beginning to make sense!"

Well, maybe, just maybe you or I can identify with either Lucy or Charlie Brown's dilemma. That is, as the one clobbered or the one doing the clobbering. Indeed, making peace is many times more difficult than making war. Peace is harder to keep than war is to fight. Recorded history speaks eloquently of this reality. It is the reconstruction, reconciling process after a confrontation that can make one painfully aware of the bitterness left behind.

Troubled times bring new opportunities to rediscover an inner peace and perhaps mend torn relationships and past misunderstandings. In a world that is anything but peaceful we can set a personal standard for a life of inner peace that is characterized by a spirit of forgiveness and reconciliation.

However, when it comes to finding personal peace, how do you do it? After all, peace must be internal before it can be external.

Well, I believe that peace must be pursued. It must be worked-at. One must strive for inner peace. Go after it. Chase it, vigorously! Seek out reconciliation and eliminate the roots of any bitterness or inner turmoil. Even if your overtures for peace are rejected you can have the inner peace that comes from knowing that you have sincerely tried to make things right. The consequences for not pursuing this inner peace will rob you of much needed energy. Lack of inner peace will dissipate you and rob you of opportunities to develop your life in positive ways. Inner turmoil can put you in a "survival" mode and can make you bitter about life and about experiences.

When bitterness is operative it becomes easier to rationalize choices that are immoral and unethical. When bitterness takes root, we can start to walk a very thin line between the truth and a lie. We can become "double-minded" giving up long term gains and pursue immediate choices that will not produce good fruit.

A story is told of three men adrift at sea who find a bottle with a genie in it. Naturally, the genie grants each one a wish. One selects a condo in the Bahamas and the other a chateau on the Riviera. They're both granted. The third man requested the following with great bitterness: "My neighbor has a goat but I am just as good a man as he is and I have no goat. I want you to kill his goat!" Imagine that! This man faces possible death and he still struggles with bitterness in his heart. Moral of the story: Bitterness can pursue us to our deathbed.

In Robert Fulghum's excellent book All I Really Need to Know I Learned in Kindergarten (Villard Books, 1988), there is a time-less quotation: "Peace is not something you wish for; it's something you make, something you do, something you are, and something you give away!"

Here's an even more timeless and timely quote for times of con-flict: "Blessed are the peacemakers, for they will be called sons of God." (Matthew 5:9)

•✚• *We have this hope as an anchor for the soul, firm and secure.*

*(Hebrews 6:19)*

## THE ANCHOR OF THE SOUL

FOR MOST PEOPLE hope carries the idea of wishful thinking. However, there is quite a distinct difference between the two. Allow me to explain.

A handsome middle-aged man had been a widower for fourteen months. His friends advised him to make some positive changes and do some new and interesting things. He took their advice and went on a seven-day cruise to the Eastern Caribbean. While walking on the deck one morning he walked past a very attractive lady about his age. She smiled at him. At that moment something jumped inside his heart. That evening he noticed her again at the dining room. She was sitting alone. He approached her and asked permission to join her for supper. In the course of conversation, he brought up the question: "Why did you smile at me today?" "Because you bear a strong resemblance to my second husband," she replied. "Oh, how many times have you been married?" he asked. "Once" she answered. Now, that is wishful thinking!

There's also the example of the little girl who stashes away hundreds of sugar cubes because she was "hoping" for a horse. That is wishful thinking! There are those that are hoping against hope that the economy will improve after blindly investing thousands of dollars into the stock market. That is wishful thinking.

Hope is the anchor of my soul. Of all the abstract realities that keep my life in motion, hope is one of the indispensable items!

If you take someone's wealth, you'll just hinder him. If you undermine someone's purpose, you'll slow her down. But, if you destroy a person's "hope," you'll stop him cold.

The Nazis in his native Germany arrested Protestant Theologian Jürgen Moltman during WWII. He spent several years in a prison camp. Here's his observation: "A man cannot live without hope. Those who lost hope in the camp lay down, took ill and died. When life's hope flounders a sadness beyond comforting sets in." (*Theology of Hope*, Fortress Press 1967)

Therefore, I must have "hope" to survive and succeed. When my hope leads me to the fulfillment of a goal or life's dream, my hope must then launch me beyond that accomplishment to dream new dreams and reach new goals.

OK, so what is hope? Well, you can start with a dictionary definition as follows: "To desire with expectation of obtainment" (Merriam Webster's Collegiate Dictionary, 10th Edition). The dictionary's approach tends to be general and bland but it's a start. I will expand on this definition by stating that true hope is that, but also much more. I believe that hope is an essential characteristic of the soul that reaches beyond me to a power which is greater and that does not change. There is only one unchanging being and that being is God. My hope must be anchored on that which does not change because everything else around me is changing, including me. If God is unchanging, then so are his promises and that gives me hope. It gives me power to live, to strive, to achieve. If I truly believe in God's unchanging character and his unchanging love (Psalm 23) then my hope will be invaded by God's unchanging purpose for me. That purpose is founded on God's very best for my life. My journey and adventure are to seek out and decide in favor of that which is right, good and pleasing. This hope, this anchor will hold in the storms of life. Because of this you and I cannot lose. True hope is a win-win proposition.

> ✦ *Do not those who plot evil go astray? But those*
> *who plan what is good find love and faithfulness.*
> *(Proverbs 14:22)*

## "GOOD" ... TO GO

THE SUNDAY SCHOOL lesson was about being good. The teacher had been illustrating different concepts of what it means to be "good" to a group of 8 to 10-year-old children. She thought she was at that moment to test the class (the teachable moment). The teacher proceeded to say to the children: "suppose you walk down the street and find a purse containing $10,000. What will you do?" The children looked wide-eyed at each other. Finally, one child spoke: "If it belongs to a poor family, I'll return it!"

It appears that the definition of "goodness" can change from person to person. What is good for one may not be an adequate definition for another. However, I would suggest that becoming "good" in the purest form is one of the great desires in our lives. I believe that we want to be good and experience it in its fullest expression.

"He's a good man!" is a common expression. But, what do we mean? After all, how "good" am I? At my funeral will people walk past my casket and exclaim "He was a good man." How will they mean it? I mean, how really good are we?

To start answering this question we must determine the difference between our individual concepts of goodness and an absolute standard of goodness. The Jews of antiquity resolved the dilemma by singing about it. They would access an ancient song that has been passed down to us over the centuries. We don't know what the music sounded like, but we do have the words:

"Blessed is the man who walks not in the counsel of the ungodly,
Nor stands in the path of sinners,
Nor sits in the seat of the scornful;
But his delight is in the law of the Lord,
And in his Law, he meditates day and night." (Psalm 1:1-2)

It must have been a catchy tune. Indeed, it was popular enough to be repeatedly sung and passed down generation to generation. The words constitute a godly definition of what it means to live the "good" life. Its poetic construction is descriptive of those that have discovered the "good." Notice that it has nothing to do with how many "toys" we own but has everything to do with developing a moral heart and wise discernment. Like all popular tunes its message is simple to understand. Its application to personal life is also practical. That is, the good avoids the bad.

The good will not walk in the council of the "ungodly." To "walk" is to order your life according to a plan, a precept or a person. It becomes the daily expression of your life. Therefore happy (blessed) is the person who will avoid the places not conducive to wholesome living and high thinking. To whom do we listen? Who are the dominant influences in our lives? The advice is compellingly clear. It links our happiness to the good council of those who walk in the proper paths and excludes the council of those who do not.

The good will not stand in the way of sinners. To "stand" is to adopt the lifestyle of another. In this case it is adopting those patterns that make us insensitive to immoral ideas that in time become socially acceptable. If we don't stand in the way of sinners, then I'm moving in the direction of God. We will be happier (blessed) in life if we don't station ourselves with those who will dull our spiritual awareness.

The good will not assume the posture of the scornful. Scornful living is the seat of arrogance and pride. It is an attitude of the spirit that leads us to be mocking, cynical and contemptuous of God and others. Scoffers are un-teachable not because they're dumb. The arrogant are un-teachable because they have resolved in their hearts to be their own god! The good will avoid these practices because the song doesn't end there. To be sure, the song is accompanied by a promise for those wise enough to apply its good advice:

> "He (she) shall be like a tree
> Planted by the rivers of water,
> That brings forth its fruit in its season,
> Whose Leaf also shall not wither;
> And whatever he (she) does shall prosper." (Psalm 1:3)

Now, I like this tune!

Billy Graham's delightful illustration sheds further light. It's the story of an old Eskimo who had trained two dogs to fight each other on his command. The Eskimo would take bets and would always win. People demanded to know how he always knew the winning dog. He always foreknew the winning dog because he would feed one dog and starve the other. Moral of the story: "the dog I feed wins." It's a matter of choice.

The bottom line is that the "good" is a matter of personal choice. I can choose "the way" or not. I can choose to delight in God's good favor or not.

⁘ *Above all else, guard your heart, for it is the well-spring of life.*

*(Proverbs 4:23)*

## HEART CONDITION

A BURGLAR WAS arrested and brought before a judge. His defense consisted of pointing out to the judge that his whole body was not involved in the burglary. The burglar insisted that only his arm and his hand had been involved. Although he freely admitted that his arm and hand took something that did not belong to him, it would be unfair of the judge to punish his whole body. The judge wisely solved the problem by sentencing the arm and hand to six years in prison while leaving it up to the rest of the body to decide whether it chose to accompany them.

Yes, it is a silly story. However, I think that it is a good illustration of what happens when we try to fragment our lives. I especially want to address this article to young single adults who many times find themselves "fragmented" in life. That is, somehow thinking that what we do in one area of life cannot possibly affect other areas. It is an approach to living that creates compartments or segments without considering the effects on the whole person.

As this mode of living persists, the young single adult may feel that he/she is getting pulled in all kinds of different directions morally, emotionally and spiritually. The temptation to rationalize and further fragment your life will cause confusion, lack of credibility and in some cases emotional imbalance. Like the cat burglar, you may find yourself on the horns of a dilemma realizing that each decision you make influences the "whole" of your life. In fact, some decisions have the power to permanently alter the rest of your life.

An anatomy of life discloses that to live healthy lifestyles you cannot "fragment" it or "compartmentalize" it. To live wholesome lives there must be unison, a coordination of good thinking, accompanied by healthy language and wholesome living. It is called integration. It means that your moral, emotional, spiritual as well as your physical life must work together in a singular integrated conviction. This translates to living lives of integrity and personal credibility.

Is this easy to do? No! But anything that was ever worth doing right has never been easy. To begin with, there are just too many distractions competing for your attention. Where to begin?

Well, from the writings of antiquity comes a tried and true piece of advice: "above all else, guard your heart for it is the wellspring of life" (The Holy Bible, book of Proverbs Chapter 4, verse 23).

I think this requires some interpretation because in antiquity, the heart was not anatomically understood the way it is understood today. Rather, the heart represented the seat of understanding and decision making. It is what modern psychology describes as the psyche, the conscious self, the center of our will and reason, the seat of the character. If you can "guard your heart," then you can guard the seat of your personality.

In this context, your heart is made up of two inclinations. The first inclination is to be rebellious and despise warning. The second, is to do what is right in pleasing God and serving your fellow man. What influences the heart? Whatever enters through the senses. Your heart, then, becomes the inner temple of your "self."

If you are beginning to feel lost in the moral jungle of contemporary society; if you sense that the standards for living are loose and the ethics for proper decision-making are confusing…

Remember: Guard your Heart!

 

 

> ⊹ *Be still and know that I am God; I will be exalted*
> *among the nations, I will be exalted in the earth.*
> *(Psalm 46:10)*

 

## Meditation: A Longing for God

DURING THE FOURTH century A.D. countless hundreds of men and women known as ascetics practiced extreme forms of spiritual disciplines. They felt that these disciplines would help them to escape temptation and other worldly distractions. In their search for holy living and spiritual renewal they would deny themselves creaturely comforts, punish their bodies and live as hermits. Some of the practices were absolutely extreme. Let me share with you some documented examples:

- A monk named Besarion would not give in to his body's need for restful sleep. For forty years he did not lie down while sleeping.

- Macarius the Younger sat naked in a swamp for 6 months until mosquito bites made him look like a victim of leprosy.

50

- Another individual spent eleven years in a hollowed-out tree trunk.

Others lived in caves, dry wells or even tombs. For them, extreme forms of discipline were the means for achieving holy lifestyles. These people were a product of their times. Indeed, their zealous commitment left its mark on the history of religion.

So, it is not surprising that when we moderns hear some statement, which refers to the practice of "spiritual disciplines", we would tend to reject those notions. What immediately come to mind are those extreme and austere images of the ancient ascetics.

However, there is a place for the practice of the spiritual disciplines in contemporary times. Given the overabundance of superficiality in relationships, spirituality and the workplace, the spiritual disciplines can do much in creating depth and sensitivity to personal improvement. But not to worry, I will not be promoting severe forms of bondage or self-flagellation. The fact is that the spiritual disciplines of prayer, meditation, worship and simplicity can do much to enhance and streamline our over-complicated lives.

Yes, modern life may make it difficult to practice the spiritual disciplines, but it is not impossible. There is good news! You don't need to be a theologian or clergy in order to practice the spiritual disciplines. All you simply need is a longing after the things of God.

In this article I'd like to address the spiritual discipline of "meditation." Meditation, or the inner world of contemplation, is how we set aside time to be alone and fill our minds with the good things of God. It is a time set aside to dispel the distractions and pressures of the present moment and allow our minds to be renewed and transformed as we openly contemplate over God's good grace and providential care over us.

In his book, *Celebration of Discipline*, Richard Foster shares some guidelines that can be helpful in developing a meditative life as follows:

1. Find a proper time: Whether one is a beginner or a seasoned veteran, it is important to set aside a time in which to practice this discipline of "holy leisure."

2. Find a place: Identify a space which is free from interruptions. This will allow you to assume a posture in which the body, mind and spirit are as relaxed as possible.

3. Center the mind: Reading a short portion from the Scriptures is recommended. Reading from the Psalms, Proverbs, and the Gospels are always good selections.

Here are a few other things to meditate over:

- God can do a lot with your life.

- God is more interested in the condition of your spirit than in the balance of your bank account.

- God just desires our willingness to follow him.

- ✢ *When you fast, do not look somber as the hypocrites do, for they disfigure their faces to show men they are fasting.*

*(Matthew 6:16)*

## Fasting: A Holy Exercise

(Please Note: Fasting is not for everyone. It is recommended that you consult with your physician
before engaging in a fast).

Over the years alcoholics anonymous type groups have flourished across America. Their success is due to their effectiveness in
providing support, encouragement and accountability among those
that seek to eliminate compulsive behaviors.

At one such meeting of Overeaters Anonymous the participants
hold each other accountable by sharing with each other how their
week has gone. One particular lady proudly shared her week by
stating: "well, this past week I exercised moderately, shopped moderately, lived moderately and ate moderately!" "Mary," the group
leader asked, "is there anything else you would care to add?" "Yes!"
she confessed, "I lie excessively!"

American society is by far one of the most food and weight
conscious society on the planet. We are the best fed country in the
world and have the weight to prove it. We generate well over fifty
percent of the entire world's food production and are strong believ-
ers in the "three square meals a day" ethic. So, with all this overabundance symbolized by the shrines to the golden arches and the
pizza temples that surround us, what are we to make of the spiritual discipline of fasting?

Well, much can still be said of fasting if we can understand its
value for spiritual formation. Please be aware that if you are looking
for a quick weight loss plan or a magical formula for achieving your
desires, fasting is not for you. If you seek to use fasting as a way of
manipulating the opinion or actions of others, then fasting is not
for you. But if you are looking for a gateway to heighten your spir-

itual awareness, dependency and focus on the things of God, then fasting may be for you.

If you plan to fast for spiritual reasons I strongly urge you to consult with your designated faith group minister. I would like to offer a definition (the what), identify the purpose (the why) and suggest some methods (the how) for fasting.

DEFINITION*: VERY SIMPLY, fasting is the abstaining from food for a spiritual purpose. It is distinguishable from hunger strikes that seek to influence political outcomes and draw attention to oneself. Fasting for spiritual reasons is also distinctly different than health dieting and weight control programs. It is typically a private matter between the individual and God.

PURPOSE: GENERALLY, THOSE who fast for spiritual reasons seek after a fuller understanding of God's direction and purpose in their lives. The primary motivation is centered on God and one's desire to better understand the things of God. In fasting one should also undergo an examination of the conscience and seek to control those negative feelings and emotions (such as pride, jealousy, hatred, etc.) that may be operative and tend to drain one's positive energy.

METHODS: AGAIN, IT its recommended that you first consult with your health care provider. The rule of thumb in fasting is "learn to walk before you run." There are three basic methods as follows:

1.   PARTIAL FAST – Start the day with a normal break-
     fast and consume fruits and juices throughout the

---

\*      *Source: Richard Foster's Celebration of Discipline,
       Harper Collins Publishers 1998*

rest of the day. Do this perhaps once a month at your discretion.

2. NORMAL FAST – After acclimating to a partial fast the body may be ready for a normal fast which abstains from food and beverages. Water is permitted. Again, one builds up to this gradually. Many people opt for a normal fast by doing it for 12 hours & gradually building up to 24 hours over a period.

3. ABSOLUTE FAST This is rarely practiced. People that engage in this are very experienced in the discipline of fasting and only exercise it under exceptional circumstances. Not recommended for beginners.

During fasting, one should perform their regular duties. One should begin their period of fasting in prayer and close their fast in prayer. Throughout the fast, reading and meditating on selected passages of the sacred scriptures is strongly encouraged. Making journal entries is also a common practice.

# SECTION III
## SPIRITUAL RENEWAL

 *Do not be anxious about anything, but in every-thing, by prayer and petition, with thanksgiving, present your requests to God.*

*(Philippians 4:6)*

### TALKING TO GOD

I AM A NOTORIOUS channel surfer. My wife and children will testify to this. I remember madly surfing through a number of channels one weekday afternoon in 1998 and coming to a quick stop when I ran across a very familiar face. It was Larry King, America's foremost interviewer. What captured my attention was that this time the role was reversed. In this particular program, Larry King was not the interviewer. Rather, he was the interviewee and what a revealing interview it was!

Mr. King was talking about his new book, *Powerful Prayers* (Renaissance Books, Los Angeles, 1998). In the process, he was revealing aspects of his spiritual beliefs. He confessed to being an agnostic and having a sense of disconnection from God (if there is one). Mr. King expressed his ambiguity about an "after-life." He expressed envy for those who pray with the assurance of being heard. However, in his book he does confess that he prayed once:

"I prayed during the 1949 World Series when the Brooklyn Dodgers faced their uptown rivals, the New York Yankees. That year, every Dodgers fan prayed for victory but we all discovered, much to our disappointment, that God was a Yankees fan – the Dodgers lost four games to one. The Yankees outplayed us and the Yankees fans out-prayed us. I made the mistake of relating this story to Rabbi Katsof during our first meeting about this book in the dining room of the Plaza Hotel.'Mr. King, God isn't a Las Vegas slot machine. You don't deposit a prayer in return for a payoff.'"

I was impressed by Mr. King's transparency on this issue. I went out and bought his book. His candor revealed a personal longing to understand one of the great mysteries of the spiritual life. To be sure, prayer is a marvelous privilege. It is a unique language of the heart that launches the believer into the very presence of God. Unfortunately, it is a privilege too often neglected.

For those of us who practice the discipline of prayer, it can pose a couple of interesting challenges. For instance: Have you ever felt frustrated or unable to find the right words while praying? Have you ever fallen asleep while praying? Have you ever felt powerless or even spiritually impotent while praying? I submit to you that this is good! It is good because it is precisely at this point of weakness that the Spirit of the Almighty can help us to pray.

If we understand our weakness and become like little children before the presence of God, God will hear our prayer, interpret it and translate it. Only God will know what we need even when we may not know ourselves.

Do you feel frustrated? Pray the prayer of frustration. Do you feel speechless? Pray the prayer of silence. Sometimes we need to be quiet long enough to hear God's "still small voice." Do you feel joy? Pray the prayer of joy! God will take our language, interpret, and translate it into spiritual power.

In prayer, the mask is down. Speak your heart to God. Don't worry about awkward words. Don't worry about waxing eloquent. Don't even worry about looking good or smelling good. God understands the inadequacy of our language and translates it into the language of the spirit.

Does God answer prayer? All the time! God's answer may be "yes", "no", "not yet" or there may be silence. If we don't understand this we may start acting like a bunch of spoiled kids.

Yes, I will pray with an active faith. I will pray in the power of God's spirit. But, I will not insult God by telling him what to do. "God's will be done" needs to be the foundation of our prayer. By praying in this manner we prepare to live within God's will.

Richard Foster in his book *Celebration of Discipline* states "Prayer catapults us into the frontier of the spiritual life" (Harper, San Francisco, 1998).

⳨ *So then, each of us will give an account of himself to God.*

*(Romans 14:12)*

## "NOT RESPONSIBLE FOR"

WE HAVE ALL seen those "not responsible for" signs in restaurants. We may also have seen the disclaimers at some high-priced parking lots. Perhaps we've read the small print on our airline tickets by which the airline assumes no responsibility for delays or missed connections. If luggage is lost, the airline may agree to pay an amount which substantially limits their liability and undervalues our lost property. These disclaimers have become symbols of a culture of irresponsibility. In short, people generally do not want to assume responsibility even for their own actions and decisions. We like to blame others so much that there is an entire legal industry built around victimization. People cash-in on blaming others to the extent that some have been known to sue municipalities for something as ridiculous as falling over their own shoelaces. Don't get me wrong, I'm all for legal remedies for obvious acts of negligence and malicious intent. What I take exception to is this culture of denying personal responsibility. The late-great comedian Flip Wilson used a comical expression when trying to place responsibility on someone else: "The devil made me do it." Indeed, some may go to the extreme of placing responsibility on God for their own indiscretions and faulty self-centered decisions, also known as "SIN."

Yes, I am going to take a big risk here and address a topic that may at best bore some and at worst offend others. You see, "Sin" is one of the most bothersome topics to address these days not just because the depth of the subject is difficult but simply because people do not want to take responsibility and would much rather blame others. Related to this is the equally compelling challenge as to what to do with "Sin" once it is recognized for what it is. My personal experience has been that when we decide to take personal responsibility, God can start working in our lives.

By the way, just a little side note on sin as I submit a simple definition. I would like to propose that sin can be simply defined as a sense of separation from God. This separation from God is an organic condition that all human beings live with. If this is the case, then "Sin" is not only related to particular actions but is rather a condition inherent in people which then leads to thoughts and actions which are inconsistent with God's good wishes. Let me illustrate: A mother of eight children had been visiting the neighbor next door and had left the children alone. She returned after the visit and to her horror realized that the kids were huddled in the center of the living room. The children had gathered around a family of skunks. The mother screamed: "Run, children, run!" Each child grabbed a skunk and ran. You get the picture?

Now, we're all running around with this "skunk." The skunk is this sinful nature we all possess. Every once in a while the skunk wants to stink up the place. That is, something or someone may entice us to either say or do the wrong thing and we will find ourselves ensnarled by a bad decision.

However, there is no need to despair. There is practical wisdom that can be applied in preventing those moments of weakness. It starts with a very simple advice expressed by no other than Socrates when he articulated the following: "Know yourself." To be sure, if we know ourselves then it should be easy to identify those things that entice us to do what is wrong. We should be able to identify those temptations that move us to entertain unhealthy thoughts. This is important because as an unhealthy desire is conceived it lodges itself in the mind and thought can easily turn into action. As we come to know ourselves we can practice the discipline of being transformed by the renewing of our minds.

Be assured that God wants to give us every good gift that comes from "above." We can't live perfect lives but we can come to clearly see those things that entice us and seek to destroy the joy of living in relationship with God. Let's talk about that some time!

·✢· *God made him who had no sin to be sin for us,*
*so that in him we might become the righteous-*
*ness of God.*

*(2 Corinthians 5:21)*

## "Mia Culpa, Mia Culpa"

During The dark days of the Cold War an archeological expedition headed by Soviet scientists were given a mummy by the Egyptian government. They carefully prepared it for shipping and sent it back to the Soviet Union for further study. Among other things, the scientists wanted to determine the mummy's age. But the scientists were rudely pushed aside by the notorious Soviet secret police (KGB) who insisted, "Leave it to us; we'll find out." After a few days the secret police made the astounding announcement that the mummy's age was 3,402 years. "That is amazing comrades," cried the Soviet scientists. "How did you ever determine it?" "That was easy," reported the secret police. "The mummy confessed."

I know…it's a lousy joke but there is a moral to the story: A little confession is good for the soul! Please, don't get me wrong. I'm not promoting some sectarian form of "confession."

I am not espousing a ritualistic or formal religious expression of the practice of confession. However, if the formal, religious form appeals to the reader…then practice it, and do so faithfully, by all means!

What I am promoting here is the practice of "dumping." That is, we all need a place to go unload. We all need a "confessional" and a "confessor." All of us, religious, non-religious (chaplains included), need a place to go and express our deepest longings, our profoundest desires and sometimes our deepest fears. This soul-purging or mental enema (be careful with that one) can do much to lighten our burden and identify new opportunities to either begin again or find new energies for the journey.

However, this should not be a one-way monologue. We must not just "speak into the wind." At the receiving end of this confessional expression, there must be a receptive ear. There must be a listener who has genuine concern for us. A diary or a journal may be a good place to record feelings, experiences and thoughts. But monologue must turn into dialogue.

This person (your confessor) should be a person handpicked by you. It should be a person that has proven their loyal friendship. He or she should be a person that has demonstrated maturity and wisdom in their speech and actions. Your trusted friend should not be a "yes" man/woman. In other words, allow that person to "agree to disagree" if necessary. Make sure that your "listener" has your permission to offer his/her advice. This should not be a judgmental person. Allow your trusted friend to freely offer an opinion and sometimes to clearly point out to you if what you are thinking or doing is right or wrong. However, do not necessarily expect advice (nor demand it). Sometimes it is just good to have someone "listen" to us attentively. Being able to just speak and be heard can be comforting. One other thing, make sure and be confident that your thoughts will be guarded and kept in the strictest of confidence.

There is a general consensus among clergy and mental health professionals that "confessing" is good (for the soul). Note that there can be some downside for not exercising this opportunity. These may be some of the negative effects when we "bottle up" thoughts that need to be expressed:

- Feelings of being overwhelmed by the conditions of life.

- Making bad decisions and further complicating our perceived problems.

- Possible depression by holding back and not seeking guidance.

- In extreme cases entertaining unhealthy thoughts that seek to truly diminish, if not eliminate, our potential for happiness and success in life.

My experience has been that confession with a trusted confidant can be an additional way to experience the grace of God. God works through people. And, oh by the way, be prepared to lend a listening ear for someone who may need to unload.

✦ *If we confess our sins, he is faithful and just and will forgive us our sins and purify us from all unrighteousness.*

*(1 John 1:9)*

## GETTING OUT THE STINK

ARE YOU A clean freak or are you more like Charlie Brown's friend, Pigpen? In centuries past, particularly the Middle Ages, people tended to be more like pigpen. That's because they considered taking a bath hazardous to their health. Back in the Middle Ages people thought that water spread the bubonic plague and other deceases. Bathing was literally considered a dangerous activity because they thought that bathing would open up the pores and expose them to what they called "pestiferous vapors."

According to their theory, through bathing, germs would penetrate the skin and make them ill. As a result, people tended to take very few baths. They merely wiped their faces and hands with a cloth (and used a lot of body powder).

They did one other thing. In days of old, people tended to take great care with their clothing. So long as their exterior created an appearance of decency and cleanliness, it didn't matter if they smelled like a stable underneath. Aren't you glad that we live in a more enlightened age? ... Or, do we?

We may not like to talk about our personal faults and we may not like to acknowledge the need for a cleansing of conscience. But, from time to time it is necessary to practice some spiritual and emotional hygiene. While we may be adept at putting on the mask that all is well, inside of us the "pestiferous vapors" of the soul continue to prowl because we may be refusing to confess the three hardest words to speak in any language: "I am wrong." To acknowledge error, to admit weakness or to confess personal fault is the most difficult of human response. The exterior may look "good to go" but the interior may be in need of some preventive maintenance. Denial of personal fault can destroy relationships and hinder us with burdens that stunt our emotional and spiritual growth.

At the opening of Alcoholics Anonymous meetings, each person introduces him/herself in the following manner: "My name is _____ and I'm an Alcoholic." Now just think for a minute. What do you think would happen in our lives and in our world if we all used the same practice: "My name is _____ and I've been wrong." Now of course, I'm making an exaggeration in order to drive home a point. The point is that any pretense to personal wrongdoing would be gone if we accepted personal responsibility. We would receive a blessing. There would be a release and we would start to experience a sense of personal renewal as we make good on past wrongdoings.

So long ago now, St. Augustine wrote: "Before God can deliver us from ourselves, we must undeceive ourselves." Self-deception hinders the blessings of God and the possibilities for personal growth. Self-deception is a stubbornness that refuses to listen and learn. Self-deception is un-confessed wrongdoings (pestiferous vapors) crawling in our spirit. Living in self-deception is like living with someone who thinks that he doesn't need a bath after three months of not bathing and their skin is turning into the colors of the rainbow. While our unrepentant spirit may say: "I'll not be brainwashed!" Keep in mind that it is not a brainwashing so much as it is a "heart cleansing" that is needed.

The funny thing about all this is that the self-deceptions, the personal faults and un-confessed wrongdoings are just on "apology" away from being made right. When we apologize and assume personal responsibility for our own actions we open ourselves to forgiveness, restoration and a cleansing of the Heart!

⸭ *"It is the duty of nations as well as of men to confess their transgressions in humble sorrow, yet with assured hope that genuine repentance will lead to mercy and pardon."*
*(Abraham Lincoln: Proclamation. March 30th, 1863).*

⸭ *If my people who are called by my name, humble themselves and pray, and seek my face, and turn from their wicked ways; then I will hear from heaven, will forgive their sin and heal their land.*
*(2 Chronicles 7:14).*

## DECONTAMINATION CHAMBER

SOME OF YOU may know that science and technology is not my strong suite. So please, indulge me for the next few moments as I delve into an area that is outside my expertise (i.e., I'll be pushing the envelope).

Plutonium is a natural radioactive substance and one of the deadliest elements known to man. It can turn normal cells into cancerous cells and take your life. Therefore, we can appreciate the major breakthrough that was made a few years ago when two scientists at the University of California discovered a process for the removal of plutonium from living tissue. That is, they discovered and designed a decontamination process for those that would ever be exposed to plutonium's deadly effects. However, there is a slight catch to this radioactive cleansing. You must know that you carry the silent killer in order to do something about it.

A similar case can also be made for proper sterilization procedures. That is, before any type of surgery there must be a proper cleansing (sterilization) of the surgical instruments as well as the human body. An improper cleansing can kill the patient. Again, there is a slight catch. You must know about the presence of bacteria in order to do something about it.

Another case can be made for the importance of proper personal hygiene. Keeping a clean body is a sound habit that will contribute to a healthy lifestyle (and happy Friendships). Yet, still there is a catch. We must know that we are dirty to effect a proper cleansing.

Today, the military is rightly concerned about the importance of decontamination, sterilization and proper personal hygiene. Indeed, these delicate areas contribute to the preservation of life.

Long ago, God showed us the more critical need for spiritual decontamination, sterilization and hygiene. To be sure, as God reveals his utter holiness I am reminded that God is holy and I am not! Personally, I am shaken by this reality. For if God is truly holy then I must see myself for who I really am. Before God's holiness I am broken, shaken and filled with self-doubt. I then must ask myself. "Do I truly love God in all His holiness?" I'm Afraid that the answer is equally frightening. I realize that I don't really, fully love God the way that I should.

In my less than perfect love for God, I have learned that my relationship with the Almighty is not based on the merits of my love for God. Indeed, it is based on the merits of God's unconditional love for me. Again, God is utterly holy and I am not!

So, here's the catch. I still have a need for a cleansing, a spiritual decontamination, as I seek to be closer to God and more fully experience God's love. It is a personal need for a cleansing that only God can provide. It is God's decontamination chamber. In Fact, not much else can happen unless this takes place. God's provision of personal confession fulfills a longing of the heart to experience a release so one can commence to more fully savor the love of God. This personal confession before God is a personal acknowledgement of my brokenness before the presence of God's utter holiness.

Long, long ago God showed a people their need for a spiritual decontamination. To the people of Israel The Tabernacle was a marvelous house of symbols and worship. As the worship center for the people of God it served as a tangible, material reminder of God's holiness, their need (and ours as well) for forgiveness and God's provision of restoration.

⋅✛⋅ *When he came to his senses, he said, "how many of my father's hired men have food to spare, and here I am starving to death!"*

*(Luke 15:17)*

# A THEOLOGY OF FORGIVENESS

IN RESEARCHING THIS topic, I ran across a time magazine article (9/23/74) that seemed to fit better in the pages of a theology journal. Those were difficult days for our country. The events were challenging the heart of our constitutional democracy and many Americans could not believe or understand how such a thing could happen in our country. The Watergate crisis was fresh in people's minds and President Nixon had resigned. Subsequently an unconditional pardon had been offered to former President Nixon by then President Ford in an effort to put the issue to rest. Time magazine picked up on the events and featured an article entitled: "A Theology of Forgiveness."

In essence, the article made a strong statement criticizing President Ford's pardon of Nixon. "The pardon, for all its compassion is bad theology." …And it went on, "Genuine pardon requires genuine confession." Indeed! Perhaps unknowingly the author of the article had drawn from the wisdom of the ages the essence of what it means to repent and be forgiven. The practical nature of the article still resonates in contemporary times. Unrepented guilt under- mines relationships and careers as people dodge personal responsibility while others refuse to extend forgiveness to the repentant and live with the burden of personal resentment.

Repentance (accepting responsibility) and Forgiveness (granting a pardon) are two sides of the same coin. Having one in the absence of the other will create distortions. Preaching repentance without receiving forgiveness creates a life driven by guilt. Offering forgiveness in the absence of repentance undermines personal accountability.

One of the greatest stories ever told by the greatest teacher that ever taught is found in the famous parable of the Prodigal Son. In this biblical account found in the 15th chapter of the Gospel according to St. Luke, a young man comes to savor the power that repentance and forgiveness play in restoring a person's life. Its message is universal, for anyone of us can become the proverbial "prodigal." Any one of us can come to experience forgiveness or extend a pardon in restoring a relationship. In the account, a young man who had acquired his inheritance and squandered it had come to his senses and returned to his father's home confessing his life of excess. The father, discerning his son's sincere repentance, forgives and restores him. A relationship is healed, and a new breath of life reanimates them.

Practicing repentance and forgiveness are essential spiritual disciplines. They are disciplines because they are not easy and demand humility and courage on our part.

- The language of repentance does not blame someone else for our shortcomings.

- The language of repentance places responsibility on the shoulders of the repentant. And…

- The language of repentance commits to a new life.

When we truly repent we come to our senses.

- The language of forgiveness does not demand revenge.

- The language of forgiveness does not denigrate the value of the repentant.

And lastly:

- The language of forgiveness seeks to restore a relationship and establish a new environment.

Repentance and Forgiveness: Two sides of the same coin and critical factors in healthy relationships.

# SECTION IV
## TAKING CARE OF BUSINESS

*·✦· For God did not give us a spirit of timidity, but a*
*spirit of power, of love and of self-discipline.*
*(2 Timothy 1:7)*

## HERE'S POWER TO YOU!

THE ABILITY OF man to harness, direct and control the energy
found in nature has enabled tremendous leaps in progress and
technology. Even the simplest discoveries and inventions have revolutionized our lives all due to man's capacity to use nature's innate
force. Yet we take so much of it for granted. Just think about it. It
only took 60 years from the Kitty Hawk's virgin flight to the Apollo
space missions. A quick nine years elapsed between NASA'S initial
plans and the actual moon-landing. Since that first landing on the
moon we have successfully landed unmanned spacecrafts on Mars.

Since World War II knowledge has doubled every ten years.
Printed texts doubled in volume every ten to twelve years and all
this progress has been due, believe it or not, to a very simple but

absolutely revolutionary discovery going back to the dawn of civilization: the discovery of fire!

However, the discovery of this energy source has had double-edged implications. Harnessing and directing that power in positive ways has had great benefits but its misdirection has lead to disastrous results. For example, back in 1992 an arsonist swept through the state of Florida setting fire to dozens of churches. It resulted in millions of dollars of destruction, to the grief and puzzlement of many who could not understand what could drive someone to do such things.

In some measure, all of us possess the ability to utilize a force of nature in positive or negative ways. This power, properly understood and applied, can propel us to great advancement as we improve our lives and the lives of those we love. Some call it "willpower." Others may call it "divine energy" while still others may call it "the power within." Whatever you may call it, be assured that all of us possess some measure of it and utilize it, misuse it, abuse it or neglect it. Misdirection of this energy force can lead to our own detriment.

All of this comes down to making some simple decisions as to how we will individually use our energy and abilities to create positive or negative results. Sure, you may not be a rocket scientist. I'm certainly not the CEO of a Fortune 500 company but we, together, can make decisions and channel our energies in positive directions. If enough of us do it consistently and with sincerity we can affect an entire generation and the world we live in.

Allow me to suggest "seven practices of highly energetic people." Consistently and sincerely applied these practices generate positive energy and maybe even revolutionize your life.

1. WATCH YOUR WALK: What if our lives were a "walking sermon"? What if our lives truly reflected those qualities that are good and right? May we walk the talk and talk the walk.

2. REDEEM THE TIME: That is, rescue your time and make the very best use of the twenty-four hours we are given to live each day. What seeds can we plant today that will give good fruit in its season? Remember that tomorrow is not promised to us, but we can always plan on leaving behind a positive legacy.

3. DON'T BE FOOLISH: Feed your mind with those things that are healthy and lead to fruitful living. Whatever feeds our thought-life will ultimately influence the way we live out our existence. Remember that if something seems too easy, it is usually either illegal or immoral.

4. DON'T GET DRUNK … with power, wine and addictions.

5. BE FILLED WITH AN AWARENESS OF GOD'S ABIDING LOVE AND PROTECTION. It will affirm your confidence and purpose in life. Whenever you sense that something is keeping you going during difficulties, be assured that there is someone (God) that's doing the "holding-up".

6. ADDRESS ONE ANOTHER WITH WORDS OF ENCOURAGEMENT AND AFFIRMATION.

7. FINALLY, BE THANKFUL. Live life with a sense of thanksgiving for the opportunity we have been given today to make a difference.

⁜ *Jesus answered, "If you want to be perfect, go, sell
your possessions and give to the poor, and you will
have treasure in heaven. Then come, follow me."*
*(Matthew 19:21)*

## SHOW ME THE MONEY

HAVE YOU SEEN the cartoon in which a man is running from his
burning house carrying his golf clubs worth $2,000? As he runs
by the firemen he says: "quick, somebody, please…get in there and
rescue my wife!" (Don't take it personal, golf lovers.)

While humorous, it really says a lot about the man, doesn't it?
It says a great deal about the condition of his heart, about what is
important to him and about what his beliefs and priorities are. The
man depicted here made a public testimony about his relationships,
his priorities and even his sense of compassion.

If finding ourselves in similar circumstances what would our
reaction be? What kinds of statements would we be making about
the stuff that we own and about "how" we own our things?

What will be our public testimony about our relationships, priorities and our sense for compassion and generosity? Yes, I'm going
to write about money and personal possessions. But, not to worry!
I will not be soliciting you. I am not on a fund-raising campaign
(Navy Chaplains are not allowed, thank God). But I am interested
in bringing to our attention an area that is near and dear to our
American way of life: owning stuff and spending money.

I will start by getting really close and personal: our 2017 Income
Tax Return. Now I'm sure that you are thrilled that each year most
of us manage to survive the ravages of the tax season. Economic
data would suggest that the average American tax payer works

the first three to four months of the year simply to pay taxes. So now that most of us are making the money I would like to make an appeal and maybe even challenge our sense of compassion and generosity.

In fact, if my memory serves me right, Schedule A of that dreaded document has a section that reads "charitable contributions." To be sure, whatever we fill into this section will make a public statement (weak or strong) about our sense of responsibility towards those less fortunate people in our communities. Please note that our sense of generosity (or lack thereof) will make a statement about the condition of our hearts.

1.  Giving to benevolent causes says that we understand our place in the world as an instrument of God's grace. Note that giving can also be measured in personal time and the donation of other types of personal assets. We may even be reminded that giving can be an act of personal worship to our God; I personally believe that our worship of God is not complete without giving!

2.  Giving will affirm in a public way whether we are possessed by our possessions. Through giving we declare our own sense of independence from the material things that seek to entrap us in a cycle of selfishness and self-absorption. Giving will liberate us from the "things" that seek to possess us.

3.  Giving says that we know what our part is. Our sense of generosity and compassion will acknowledge that we assume personal responsibility for making our contribution. This also addresses the practical aspects of giving to our local community

of faith (i.e., church, temple, and mosque). It challenges us to regular and consistent giving in relation to our income.

I believe that most of us desire to be generous and compassionate. As we prepare to enter the following tax preparation season, I would like to challenge us to become more adept at contributing to works of benevolence and compassion through giving and/or volunteer work. As we do so, we will lighten the burden of those in need and make a powerful personal statement.

⟐ *No one can serve two masters. Either he will hate the one and love the other, or he will be devoted to the one and despise the other. You cannot serve both God and Money.*

*(Matthew 6:24)*

## MONEY TALKS

A MAN FELL into a frozen lake and a friend was providentially close enough to pull him out of the water. "You should give your friend at least twenty dollars for saving your life" the man's minister said to him. "Well Reverend, can I make it ten dollars? I was half dead when he pulled me out."

Hey, imagine that! He was "half dead," therefore half the cost for saving his life. Moral of the story: Money talks. In fact, do this. Take a dollar bill from your pocket and just look at it. It is disturbingly real how this inanimate piece of paper seems to take on the trappings of personality. When it goes into our pocket it becomes an extension of who we are. If you want to know some things about me, just take a few moments to review my checkbook. You see, money talks and it talks about us. We have all heard stories about people who have been ruined by money. Perhaps we personally know people who have been consumed by greed because of money.

However, the reality is that money is intrinsically neutral. Money is neither good nor bad. If money corrupts someone it is because the person was already corrupt to begin with. If money kills a person's spirituality it is because the person was spiritually lifeless already.

Our use of money will talk. Sometimes its message is about the false security we have placed in it. Money will speak volumes and sometimes can even deliver a powerful sermon. Indeed, our use of money can also reveal our personal theology. To be sure, Schedule A of our personal tax return has a line item for designating the sum total of the year's monetary donations. I submit to you that our entry on that line item will make a powerful statement about our spirit of benevolence and personal faith. God knows that money talks.

I would like to address money management from the perspective of benevolence (i.e. how we use it to help others). In one of his engaging sermons, the Rev. Charles Swindoll explained that there are three kinds of givers in the world. We could liken them to "the flint," "the sponge" or "the honeycomb."

> THE FLINT: *To get anything from the flint we must hammer at it. The result is that you get only a few chips and sparks.*

> THE SPONGE: *To get anything from the sponge, no matter how much it has absorbed, we must still squeeze and squeeze it. But............*

> THE HONEYCOMB: *It just overflows and drips with sweetness.*

I will give all of us the benefit of doubt and will assume the best. That is, we are all like the honeycomb when it comes to giving to those in need. We have a generous spirit because we realize some compelling realities about our surroundings. Indeed, we live in the most prosperous nation in the history of humanity. Even some of the less affluent among us can boast some basic creature comforts that are the envy of many people beyond our borders. Understanding this, the principle of application is very simple: "to those who have much received, much is expected." This assumed trust in our innate generosity is important because it informs us that in times of personal need we can count on each other's willingness to help. We can appeal to our collective sense of mutual trust. Our personal commitment in giving to worthwhile causes manifest our collective commitment to be generous and helpful.

I will also make two other bold assumptions. That is, I will assume God's blessings when we are faithful in our generosity (for it is more blessed to give than to receive). I will also assume "synergism" as a result. Synergism is defined as "when the whole is greater than the sum of the parts." This translates into transformation as communities are revitalized and lives are changed because of the generosity of the committed.

⁘ *For the love of money is a root of all kinds of evil.*
*(1 Timothy 6:10)*

## ROLLING THE DICE

THE STORY GOES that in Las Vegas a certain large hotel with a casino had been known to prominently and conspicuously display

$1,000,000 inside a plexiglass case. Located in the center of the main gambling floor, the display was carefully watched by an armed guard.

People approached the display and stood around it in reverential awe (some were salivating, others gawking). "Well Chaplain, how do you know about this?" You may ask. My Response: "another Chaplain told me about it!"

An enterprising company also set up offices in four Las Vegas casinos offering gamblers "same day refund anticipation loans." Few people noticed or cared when a Florida inventor was granted a U.S. patent to someday enable television audiences to legally bet on game shows or sports games from their home.

Yes! Gambling has been around for a long time. It ranks right up there with the world's oldest profession. Dices made from the anklebone of sheep have been unearthed by archeologists. Two thousand years ago Romans used the dice for gambling. In the Holy Land one can still find games of chance carved into the pavement where Roman soldiers would play their games of chance. Romans and their emperors loved to gamble, and many were compulsive. A certain Roman emperor had his chariot rigged for games. Caligula once became so furious at losing that he ordered a noble citizen executed and his estate confiscated to pay for his gambling loss. Historians observe that the Ceasers' preoccupation with gambling became a significant factor leading to the decadence and decline of the Roman Empire.

In contemporary America the Legalized gambling industry is compelling. In excess of 100 million people visit casinos every year. Over 300 Billion dollars are gambled away each year. This does not include illegal gambling, which would increase the dollar figure very significantly. Personally, I find these figures startling and beyond my imagination. Try, if you can, to imagine the tremendous capitalization for other businesses and jobs if this kind of spending power was used otherwise. But, here is where I became very concerned. It is estimated that there are about ten million Americans that are addicted to gambling. Please be assured that I am not naive enough to think that gambling should disappear. Legalized gambling is part of the landscape and, at some level, provides entertainment for a segment of the population. However, its excesses do lead to addictive behavior that is destructive to individuals and their families. At a meeting of gambler's anonymous groups, the personal stories that are shared are heart-breaking.

If you must gamble, here are some suggestions that will maintain balance and moderation:

1. Resign yourself to the reality that the odds are vastly against you. You will more than likely lose your money.
2. Limit your amount of loss. Budget the amount of money you will take to the casino. Once you have lost that money decide in advance to walk away.
3. The money you use for gambling should not be funds you use for paying bills and providing for your family.
4. Limit your amount of winnings. If you happen to be on a winning streak, decide in advanced that you will desist from gambling after accumulating a set amount.
5. Leave your credit card, ATM card and blank personal checks at home. Limit your access to cash while at the casino.
6. If you find yourself gambling excessively, don't hesitate to seek assistance.

1+1=2 in this world or any other world, it's a constant law of mathematics (in base 10). However, when applied to gambling, 1+1=0. It is a vice that defies the laws of logic and excessively practiced can lead to destructive results for individuals, and their families.

·✥· *Be very careful, then, how you live—not as unwise but as wise,*

*(Ephesians 5:15)*

## TIME: USE IT OR LOSE IT

BACK IN THE day a peddler was selling a potion, which he declared would make one live to a ripe old age. "Why, look at me!" he shouted. "Healthy, hearty, strong and energetic...I'm over three-hundred years old." A person in the crowd turned to the peddler's young assistant and asked, "Is he really as old as that?" "Well, I can't say" he answered. "I've only worked for him a hundred years."

Really...what would we do with our time if we could live three hundred years? In a way this is a ridiculous question because I know that I will not live on this earth for three hundred years. But, you know – perhaps you have found yourself, like I have, making the equally ridiculous statement: "If I could only turn back the hands of time." It's worthless, wishful thinking because I can't and yet we seek to recapture it and replay wasted time.

The truth of the matter is as follows: We're all running out of time (the chronological kind). Time is one of those commodities that when you're out of it, you're out of it! Think about it. If you run out of oxygen, you can buy some. If you run out of money you can earn some. If you are homeless you can go to a shelter. But, if you're out of time, it's gone!

All of us are enveloped in this chronological dimension that can control us. We can find ourselves running out of time for the most important people and things in our lives. We may find ourselves with never enough time for family, friends, and responsibly planning our lives. We may even find ourselves with never enough time for God. Time can become the tail wagging the dog!

I'm interested in identifying and applying some time-tested principles that will help me to be a good manager of my time and therefore, my life. So, here goes.

Walk circumspectly. I just like this expression! It's a dignified way, "old English" way of saying BE CAREFUL – BE WISE. I truly believe that time is a gift given to us by The Almighty. As recipients of this gift we are invited to be good stewards/managers of whatever block of time we have been given. I must apportion my time properly and be careful and wise to make the most of each opportunity. I must "make" the time to spend significant moments with my family. I must "make" time to block out a meeting with an old friend. I must attempt to capture those opportunities to assist, to help, to encourage a person expressing need. The irony of life is that while we may complain about the lack of time for study, family and even praying, we may find ourselves doing "nothing" from time to time.

You know, I love the study of ancient history. One of the important facts about ancient history is that everyone in it is dead. They all ran out of chronological time. As I consume and use up my portion of time I realize that one day I'm going to be dead too and I'm not even going to leave a hole. Yes, I'm also reminded that an eternal existence awaits a people of faith, but I am encouraged to know that in this place and in this time I am invited to use my time carefully!

I'm also reminded of some catchy maxims regarding time:

- "Time is money and money is profit." (True, if you're in business)

- "Time is of the essence." (True, if you're working on a deadline)

- "Time is on my side." (True, if you use it carefully)

- "Do you love life? Then do not waste time, for that's the stuff life is made of." (Benjamin Franklin).

Be Careful, Be Wise!

✢ *Then he said to them, "Watch out! Be on your guard against all kinds of greed; a man's life does not consist in the abundance of his possessions."*
*(Luke 12:15)*

## LIVING WITHIN YOUR MEANS

YOU GO TO check for the mail (snail mail). Sitting in the mailbox is this official looking letter addressed to you from the law firm of "Northam, Southern, Eastin, Westin and Fred." You open the envelope and read the contents. It contains both good and bad news. First the bad news: Your great aunt Lulu has passed away. You remember meeting aunt Lulu some twenty years back at a family reunion. You had never seen her again, but you never forgot her words: "I won't forget you, Charlie," she said.

Well, as it turns out your great aunt Lulu was a bit of an eccentric; shall we say a very eccentric "fruit-cake?" To your amazement the letter informs you that you have been named in her last will and testament!! The reading of the will takes place in two weeks at the attorney's office and your presence is requested. The next fourteen days go by very slowly. The anticipation is simply killing you. You keep dreaming about the Mercedes you will drive, the new boat you will sail and the new wardrobe you will purchase with the inheritance money. You can't sleep at night. Nothing can squelch your excitement.

The big day finally arrives. You dress in your "finest" and make the pilgrimage to the attorney's office for the reading of aunt Lulu's will. It reads as follows: "I, Mrs. Lulu McIntosh, being of sound mind and body, am richer than anyone can possibly imagine. I am leaving my entire fortune to my cats except for a few token gifts to the friends and relatives who least offended me during my lifetime. (The lawyer pauses and swallows hard). To my sister Louise I leave my complete collection of ceramic Fidel Castro figurines. To my cousin Henry I leave the ball of string that I've been collecting since 1933. To my brother James, who was always telling me that health is far more important to a person than wealth, I now leave the entire contents of my third-floor closet, my sun lamp and…to my great nephew whom I promised to remember…HI THERE CHARLIE!"

OUCH! What a cruel act of deception. But, it really has been an act of self-deception. That is usually how greed starts. We can lull ourselves into fantasizing about things that belong to us when in fact they do not. That's also how excessive indebtedness begins.

The principle here is very simple. That is, we can never claim some things that were never ours to begin with. It is all about stewardship and responsible management of our financial and material resources. You see, you and I arrived in this world naked (nothing, zilch, "nada") and will leave this world with nothing, not even our tonsils.

In the meantime, the Almighty, in all his wisdom has made us stewards, (caretakers) over a variety of things. This would include our relationships, our physical body, our family, our moral and spiritual well-being and our financial and material resources. Responsible management of our finances can be especially challenging in our consumer-driven society. It requires personal discipline in planning and personally acknowledging the limits of our spending power. Faltering in this area typically happens when we deceive ourselves into overspending and building up excessive debt.

Reality happens when we realize that there is still too much month left at the end of our paycheck. Reality happens when we realize that we can't claim some things that were never ours to begin with. The key to a responsible financial lifestyle is finding that fine balance between the use of money and its limits. To be sure, money can buy many things except love, character, freedom of the spirit and immortality.

Living within our means in the present and proper planning for financial success in the future is responsible, practical and stress-free.

⁘ *For where your treasure is, there your heart will be also.*

*(Matthew 6:21)*

## HUNTING FOR TREASURE

THE YOUNG MAN approached his minister in a spirit of confession. He did so in the hope of ridding himself of a compulsive habit that was creating a considerable amount of guilt in his life. The young man spoke to the pastor before the commencement of Sunday service. "Pastor, I'm a spendthrift. I throw my money around left and right. I don't save any of it and spend it compulsively. Sir, please pray for me during the service that I may be cured of this habit."

Identifying an opportunity, the pastor answered: "Oh yes my boy. The prayer will come right after we take up the offering." Well, maybe the church was traversing financial difficulties and the pastor resorted to a creative approach with questionable ethics. However, we would be less than honest if we were to say that finances are not important in our lives.

Indeed, there is no doubt that we live in a society that can be financially obsessed. The peculiar ways in which we handle our money will affect how we live. None of us are exempt from the temptations and pitfalls that bad money management can bring to our lives. To be sure, as a society we have learned to live beyond our means thereby creating a debtor society. Many cannot differentiate between "what we want" from "what we need." A well-known former spouse of a real estate mogul once exclaimed that she "needed" 6.2 million dollars per year to live (so do I). Really, what person "needs" $6.2 million per year to live?! I think that what she meant to say was that she "wanted" the $6.2 million as opposed to needing it.

Of course, money is important. A vital aspect of successful money management is determining balance and discerning what we "need" from what we "want". I will even go a step further and assert that there is a connection between a person's spiritual health and financial management. Let me illustrate:

If you have an interest in purchasing a piece of real estate, the practice calls for putting down some "earnest money." That is, several hundred dollars will typically tie-up a real estate contract that will protect your claim until the purchase is closed. In effect "earnest money" is another way of saying: "Put your money where you mouth is."

Now, here's the connection between spiritual health and financial management and you fill in the blank: "put your money where your _ _ _ _ _ is". If you entered "heart" you are correct ("for where your treasure is, there your heart will be also" Gospel of Mathew 6:21). This becomes a test of our authenticity, accountability and reciprocity.

Personal money management is a test of our authenticity as we learn to give of ourselves, our abilities and our resources to enrich others with the blessings we have received. We may feel rich in our faith, speech, knowledge and motivation. These things are balanced by expressing grace in giving to those with legitimate needs. It is one of those intangibles, constant principles that will always be with us, whether we believe in it or not.

How we handle our money is a test of our accountability, as we understand that sound stewardship is a sacred trust. When that sacred trust is broken through unethical, underhanded practices, the effects trickle down to others who must then carry an uneven share of the burden.

Money is a neutral commodity. It can be used for good or evil as we decide how that commodity will be best utilized. When used for good its dividends are multiplied and become a projection of our commitment to the "sacred trust."

Finally, "what goes around comes around." Reciprocity, the principle of reaping and sowing, is an intangible precept that essentially asserts that as we supply, we will be supplied. Outlandish and exorbitant lifestyles generally lead to outlandish, exorbitant debt. Balance is the key.

Our money will follow our heart.

> ⊹ *Therefore, I urge you, brothers, in view of God's mercy, to offer your bodies as living sacrifices, holy and pleasing to God—this is your spiritual act of worship.*
>
> *(Romans 12:1)*

## THE BODY IS A TERRIBLE THING TO WASTE

I THINK THAT no other period in history has more exemplified the importance that American society presently places on the care of the human body. The physical fitness industry is a multibillion-dollar business and aging baby boomers are spending exorbitant sums on "nipping and tucking" in order to preserve their youthful looks. Some economists have speculated that on average a typical American will spend $100.00 as follows: $18.30 for food, $6.60 for recreation, $5.90 for clothes, $60.00 for housing/transportation/medical, and $1.30 for religious causes. In other words, taking care of our bodies means big business. On average, we spend more time, money and effort related to our bodies than we do any other single dimension of our life. We also pay a lot of attention to the way our national celebrities take care of their bodies. And of course, there are those that study the art and science of "body language." The science of body language has taught us that the configuration, the posture and gesture of our body has a language all its own. After all, the body is visual and easy for others to understand because everyone can relate to the expenditure of the physical.

It is interesting to note that the Bible has some practical and comprehensive advice regarding our bodies. For all its marvelous spiritual and theological revelations, the Bible has much to say concerning the use of the body. Its clear teaching confirms that our body is part of our personal witness. How we treat and use our bodies will make a statement to people around us. Indeed, how we treat our bodies, use our bodies and express ourselves become a unique aspect of my personal witness. Subsequently we will have many opportunities to directly use or misuse our bodies. The Holy Scriptures challenges us to be good stewards of our body because in some respects our body can become our "calling card."

I think that the Apostle Paul was perhaps at the peak of his teaching and practical theological depth when he wrote, with great passion, "I urge you, brothers, in view of God's mercy, to offer your bodies as living sacrifices, holy and pleasing to God. This is your spiritual act of worship" (Romans 12:1). The concept of being a living sacrifice is unique to the Bible. In fact, we are challenged to make it a dominant characteristic of how we live our lives and utilize our bodies. This translates into personal discipline that begins with the mind and transfers to our emotions and to our physical body. The problem comes at the point of personal obedience. I heard a colleague once express it in the following way: "The problem with being a living sacrifice is that it has the tendency to crawl off the altar." Indeed!

However, our body is the primary material given to us by God. We are then to unconditionally give our bodies back to God for his good purposes. This, then, is a compelling, dramatic and unique calling for God's people. So, as I offer up my body to God there are a couple of practical and wise factors I can follow:

1.   We are made up of body, mind and spirit. There-
     fore, taking care of the whole person requires time,

effort and personal discipline. Finding balance, therefore, is the critical component in developing the whole person. Our body becomes a projection of our thinking and our spiritual maturity as we decide to care for it and use it wisely.

2. Don't yield your body to immoral acts. This I can control! There is a clear choice. I can either use my body for evil or for good. After all, the body is the physical extension of my soul. Given its own course, the body will self-destruct. But, if we give in to God's purpose and authority we're giving in to living a full life and the realization of God's good purpose.

Years ago, a national magazine featured the story of identical twins who had to sleep, eat and get disciplined together. As five-year olds they were literally inseparable. They could not be separated because they both shared a common heart. Friends, we simply cannot give our life to God and keep our body to ourselves. To share a common heart with the spirit of God requires, indeed demands, an abiding sense of inseparability from God. Anything short of that is incompatible with God's good purpose for our lives. Now, will we take that challenge?

> ·✢· *But store up for yourselves treasures in heaven, where moth and rust do not destroy, and where thieves do not break in and steal.*
> *(Matthew 6:20)*

## Packing for Heaven

Popular folk-wisdom says: "when preparing to travel, lay out all your clothes and all your money. Then, take one half the clothes and twice the money." This may be considered good advice from experienced travelers. Indeed, seasoned travelers will travel light. For novice travelers the temptation is to overload their bags. The goal in successful traveling is to take only that which is essential for the journey.

I think you will agree that we are all fellow travelers in the journey of life. Our travels will eventually take us to our final destination. How we pack for the journey, materially and spiritually, will have a direct impact on how we live out this journey of life. How we pack our bags will determine whether we are joyous, mediocre or just downright burdened in life's journey.

The dilemma we face many times is in trying to distinguish between our needs and our wants. Knowing the difference is important in determining the extent of the weight we bear in life. Have you noticed? It appears that the more we have, the more we tend to want. Perhaps what was once a dream has become an unreasonable obsession to possess. But should this surprise us? After all, we live in the wealthiest nation on the face of the planet! God has truly blessed our country with abundance. Even some of our poorer citizens seem wealthy when compared with the poorest of the poor in third world countries. Our affluence as a society elevates our personal expectations. It can inflate our values (and our egos). What can happen? Well, we can become confused in trying to distinguish between our needs and our wants.

To travel right and light, there are certain principles that must be considered and even mastered. We will travel light as we refuse to be weighed-down with materialism. Not to worry, I'm not asking you to give away your Rolls Royce. But, I am saying that we must control our possessions and not allow our possessions to control us. This requires a discriminating eye in identifying those things we really need. It is more a condition of the mind and heart. How we handle and manage our possessions will make a statement about the condition of our spirit. To be sure, the condition of our spiritual, moral and emotional luggage must take priority over our material things. So, what should be packed inside this spiritual, moral and emotional luggage?

Well, a few years ago an elderly friend, a member of the church where I had the privilege to be the Senior Pastor, blessed me. His name was Art Blizard and at the age of 94 he went to be with his Lord. He blessed my life with a poem written by him and filled with much common-sense knowledge about traveling right and light. I share Art's poem with you:

When we plan to go on a journey,
I'm packing love in abundance,
We pack our suitcase with care.
A little more every day.
So I'm packing my suitcase for heaven
Kind words for those all around me
For I'm counting on soon going there.
And prayers for all on life's way.
Joe says I can take nothing with me.
No hate shall go in my suitcase,
But to that I must disagree,
No jealousy, no strife or care.
For I want some heavenly baggage,
Only the pure, the true, the good
When I go my Jesus to see.

Shall ever enter there!
So I'm packing my suitcase for heaven,
I long for traveling companions
And choosing each item with care.
On this glorious heavenly way.
For my call may come unexpected
So won't you start packing your bags
And I wouldn't have time to prepare.
And join me dear Joe today?

···⊕···

# SECTION V

## THE SCHOOL OF HARD KNOCKS

···⊕··· *But he knows the way that I take; when he has*
*tested me, I will come forth as gold.*
*(Job 23:10)*

### "THIS IS A TEST...."

A MINISTER WAS making a wooden trellis to support a climbing
vine. As he hammered away he noticed a little boy watching. The
boy didn't say a word. He was just looking on. The minister kept
working, thinking that the boy would eventually leave but the child
did not leave. Thinking that the boy was admiring his handiwork
the minister paused and asked the boy: "Well son, are you trying
to pick-up some pointers on gardening?" "No," he answered. "I'm
just waiting to hear what a preacher says when he hits his thumb
with a hammer." The boy was waiting for the preacher to be tested.

We can surely measure our spiritual maturity by the way we
respond when we are faced with a test. Our reactions, whether in
words or actions, are a mirror into the soul. When I was a child,
I would associate a "test" with watching television (maybe you

remember), the screen going blank and an announcement would be heard: "This is a test of the emergency broadcast system. For the next sixty (60) seconds…." As a child, that test would always scare me. I always thought that we were on the verge of a nuclear attack from the Soviets.

"Test." The mere mention of the word can strike fear in the life of some. The slightest anticipation of facing a test can make us very conscious of our heartbeat. This may not come as particularly welcome news, but tests will happen in all our lives! Trials come along to test the mettle of our faith and the substance of our personal convictions. When tested we will discover where we stand on the essential matters of life. When tested we can either grow closer to God or farther from God.

Some people have a mistaken notion regarding the trials of life. That is, some would maintain that if we prosper and all is well, then God must be on our side. Prosperity becomes a gauge measuring God's favor. The reality is simply that sooner or later all of us are tested because that is simply the nature of life.

So, let me share with you some things I've learned from the school of hard knocks about tests (big or small).

1. Tests are designed to show whether we're learning. Past experiences prepare us for future challenges. What are the lessons learned from those experiences and will it prepare us to face future obstacles? This approach to life's tests will develop methods of preparation and enhance our maturity.

2. Be prepared for surprise quizzes. We will never know when they'll come along. We will never know what area of our life will be addressed. Therefore, let us be aware of our strengths and weaknesses and strengthen the weak areas. I've noticed that

when trials come they usually challenge us at the point of our weakness.

3. It is always an "open book test." By this I mean that during all difficulties there are always people and resources available to assist and orient us. We must identify trusted and wise friends who can provide council and keep our confidence. We must identify our deepest faith convictions and access those resources that God has given us to help us navigate through life.

There are three categories of people who are reading this article. The first category consists of those that have been tested. You can pass to others the benefits of your experiences and lessons learned.

The second category is made up of those that are in the midst of a test. I've met some of you and I know of your heroism. I know of your openness to receiving good counsel and willingness to persevere. Hang in there! God always provides a way.

The third category is comprised of those that can see a test coming at you. The questions for you: "what kind of a student are you and what preparations are you making?"

⁘ *A man's wisdom gives him patience; it is to his glory to overlook an offense.*

*(Proverbs 19:11)*

## HAVE IT YOUR WAY...NOT! (ON PATIENCE)

IT WAS TIME for me to renew my auto tag registration. But this time I had waited too long. I could no longer renew it through the mail.

In fact, my neighbor at the time, who was a police officer, kindly reminded me that I was driving with an expired tag. I suppose that his reluctance in ticketing me was his way of avoiding the wrath of God. I rushed to the department of motor vehicles and had not anticipated all the people that would be waiting in line before me. I waited for nearly one hour with the rest of this pitiful mob of humanity that found themselves in the same dilemma as I. My frustration level started shooting through the roof. My patience was wearing really thin. However, I had no one to blame for this but myself.

I made sure that all my paperwork was in order, to avoid an additional trip back. I got up to the counter and I see this huge poster behind the attendant. The poster reads: "THIS IS NOT BURGER KING. YOU DON'T HAVE IT YOUR WAY. YOU HAVE IT OUR WAY OR YOU DON'T HAVE IT AT ALL." The lady behind the counter (resembling a dreaded Drill Sergeant in appearance and tone) said in a forbidding voice "Can I help you?!" and I thought "I hope not." I transacted my business and was treated by the clerk as something to be disposed of.

As I left (with registration renewal in hand – thank God) I felt bothered by the experience and the message on the poster. I guess I was disturbed by the truth the poster expressed. Truth does have a way of disturbing us sometimes. I realized one thing…that life seems to be filled with a sprinkling of those confrontational moments. Those moments remind me that much of life can't be my way. I must do it "their way or else." In the midst of that reality there is an inner struggle of feelings and emotions. How can I learn to react? How can I learn to respond with grace to those confrontational situations which appear to be unfair and out of place? How Do I respond to a world that from time to time flashes that big sign: YOU HAVE IT OUR WAY OR YOU DON'T HAVE IT AT ALL.

For starters, I believe we must look beyond the particular negative experience and keep our eyes on "end results." In other words, I have to keep my eyes on "The Big Picture."

What's The Big Picture? The Big Picture includes knowing me. It is about having goals in life. It is about understanding my place in the world and my purpose in it. Keeping The Big Picture in sight helps us through the conflicts of life and will give us a healthier balance and perspective on life.

A critical component to The Big Picture is assuring that we set reasonable and achievable goals in life. I once heard it expressed this way: "A goal is a dream with a date on it." How many of us have The Big Picture? How many of us have goals in life? You see, once a goal is achieved, a new goal is set. It keeps The Big Picture alive.

OK, but what does this have to do with dealing with the "nasties" that life deals us from time to time? I think…everything. You see if I possess The Big Picture then the negative events are simply hurdles or obstacles that I must negotiate through (and we all know about obstacle courses).

If I can keep my eyes focused on The Big Picture I'll understand that there is a reason for everything. I may not see that amid the moment but down the road hindsight will point out to me the lesson I learned. Those negative moments can be great learning moments on the journey of life. Those learning moments are preparing and challenging us to stay focused and keep our eyes on The Big Picture.

While standing in that long line at the auto tag agency and dealing with this less than friendly clerk with an attitude and "the sign" I was learning something, mostly about myself. I was learning about the discipline of self-control. I was learning about the discipline of managing my personal affairs on a timely basis. I was learning about the discipline of patience…and patience is a virtue.

⁘ *That is why, for Christ's sake, I delight in weak-*
*nesses, in insults, in hardships, in persecutions, in*
*difficulties. For when I am weak, then I am strong.*
*(2 Corinthians 12:10)*

## PUTTING ON THE BOXING GLOVES

YES! IT WAS a ballyhoo. At the time, the event was the most pub-
licized boxing match in the entire history of the sport. It was the
World Heavyweight rematch between the then Champion, Muhammad Ali, and the top contender, Joe Frazier. This took place way
back in 1975 during the golden era of boxing with personalities
to match. In 1975 the world had already been waiting close to five
years for the rematch of all rematches. The venue for this historic
event was Manila, Republic of the Philippines. As the momentum built up, Ali himself dubbed the upcoming encounter as "The
Thrilla in Manila!" Accessibility to modern technology via satellites
made it possible for one billion people to watch worldwide. This
alone was a remarkable feat at the time. Imagine that, one third of
the world's population watched this event in awe. The clash between
these two titans had great mass appeal.

The bout lived up to every fan's expectation and then some. As
these two powerful men went at it, the match went the distance. The
fifteen rounds of blood sweat, and pain made history in the annals
of boxing. After it was over Ali simply said: "We both came close
to death." He was serious! This encounter had renewed a sense of
mutual respect in each boxer.

It has been suggested that contact sports, be it boxing, wrestling,
football etc., have such a great appeal because we can see something of ourselves in the struggle. These sport encounters become

metaphors for life as we project ourselves into the heat of battle. We can identify with the athletes as they contend with the forces around them. Whether we root for the champion or the underdog, we vicariously live through them. Their injuries become our hurt and their humiliations affect us, as we also become contenders alongside them.

Ultimately, all of us are contenders in life. As we encounter the oddities and strife of life we may find ourselves contending with our work, our families or even with God. If you are a contender in life, as I know you are, I would like to suggest a three-round amateur bout that can lead us to some discoveries and to some decisions of life-changing proportions.

ROUND 1, THE STRUGGLE: The struggles of life can lead us down the road of uncertainty. Perhaps you can relate to the uncertainty that accompanies the possibility of losing everything you've worked hard to accumulate. Struggles can render us vulnerable to thoughts of fear and feelings of loneliness. The struggle can force us to address the ultimate issues of life itself. Strife can lead us to ask questions that can help us to understand our purpose, our role and our place in this world.

ROUND 2, THE MOMENT OF TRUTH: Times of struggle provide unique opportunities to learn much about the self and our potential for growth. These moments of truth can even force us to count our blessings even amid difficulties. A good question to ask during a time of struggle is: "What am I learning through this experience? How can I become a better person through this?" If we sincerely ask those questions and sincerely attempt to answer them, we will identify that there are some diamonds in the rough waiting to be cut and polished.

ROUND 3, THE DECISION: Notice that in coming to terms with life we must also be prepared to come to terms with our God. The truth found here might be a hard pill to swallow for some. You see, when a child of God doesn't respond to the Almighty's gentle leading and persists on self destruction or fruitless ways in life we must decide. One must decide to be (or not to be) "blessed" by God. This is a decision of the will in which we posture ourselves to think, speak and act in ways that are right and pleasing to our God. The paradox lies in that the answer to our problem is, time and again, found in the act of self-surrender to the Almighty.

⊹ *Then the LORD said to Cain, "Where is your brother Abel?" "I don't know," he replied. "Am I my brother's keeper?"*

*(Genesis 4:9)*

## LIFE'S DEFINING MOMENT

A NEWSPAPER ONCE reported an unusual incident at a fast-food restaurant. The manager of the restaurant had placed the night's bank deposit in a paper bag. An attendant mistook the bag for an order and gave it to a couple at the drive-through window. Later, the couple stopped at a park to eat the contents. Upon realizing what they had, they decided to drive back to the restaurant and return the money. Meanwhile, the manager had already called the police and reported the incident as a robbery. The police and a television crew arrived at the scene at about the same time that the couple returned with the money. The manager was elated. They made his day! He went up to the couple and said, "You should be featured on the evening news for being honest!" "Oh, please, no publicity," said the man nervously…" "She's not my wife."

Wow! What a defining moment. It revealed what was hidden. The moment brought out both the good side as well as the dark side of the human spirit. What may be most intriguing to us is that we never know when one of life's defining moments may come knocking on our door.

The story of Cain and Able is one of the Bible's most compelling accounts. It was a defining moment particularly in the life of Cain as his own greed and envy towards his brother Able overwhelmed his heart. Cain's feelings of resentment towards Able lead him to commit a most heinous crime. He murdered his brother! Cain had been rendered hopeless by the condition of his heart when his decisive moment came along.

The condition of our heart will always establish the outcome of our defining moment. The Bible's account of Cain's crime reveals that just prior to his deed he had been angry and depressed. As sin was crouching at his door, his negative emotions opened the door of his heart and the tragic act of murder was conceived.

Examining the condition of our heart is critical. Are we driven by anger? Is there a tinge of hatred clinging to our emotions? Are we driven by feelings of revenge? Are there unresolved problems that continue to undermine our best efforts in trying to do the right thing? In fact, if we know God and worship God, our worship of God can be rendered unacceptable by God if the condition of our heart is not right.

Many times life's defining moment take place amid a broken heart or as we confront a terrible temptation. The defining moment will present us with two options and two options only. We will either decide to do what is right or do what is wrong. Remember, the condition of our heart will establish our defining moment. Will our response be God-centered or other-centered?

So, what is so important about the "defining moment?" After all, we're just average people trying to make our way in life. Things happen and we do the best we can. Well, that may be. Nevertheless, "defining moments" are just as important for the average person as they are for the President of the United States.

You see, defining moments are the shapers of our soul. It is through tests and challenges that our personal morals and ethics are shaped. The "defining moment" will help us identify those core values that we truly believe in. It will bring to light the real nature of our character. Eventually we will all face our defining moment(s).

If you believe that you are a person with a destiny then you will embrace the importance of life's defining moments. If you are a believer in the Living God, you will be compelled to act decisively in those defining moments. Our destiny on this planet is realized as we work together for the good of our fellow man. Our destiny is realized as we watch the condition of our heart. Our destiny is fleshed-out as we are called upon to make important personal decisions that will impact the lives of others. With the proper attitude of heart and with a grace-filled spirit we can accomplish God's good purpose, in those defining moments.

⸙ *The name of the LORD is a strong tower; the righteous run to it and are safe.*

*(Proverbs 18:10)*

## FIGHT, FLIGHT OR COOPERATE

THERE'S AN INTERESTING story about a Methodist and Baptist preachers who were fierce competitors (places and names will remain anonymous to protect the guilty). Their two churches were located across the street from each other and both churches were roughly the same size.

106

These two ministers competed for members. They competed for attention from the community. They competed on the quality of their sermons. This had caused a lot of tension between those two "men of God." A prominent and concerned citizen of the community wanted to see the two pastors get together in a spirit of cooperation and love. Therefore, he paid for both pastors to go hunting. For several days they shared everything. They shared a small tent. They cooked their meals over the same fire and a good spirit of brotherly love actually started to develop between them... until one night. An angry grizzly bear started clawing at their tent. The bear was hungry and had a bad attitude.

"Let's run for it!" said the Methodist minister.

"You can't outrun a grizzly!" yelled the Baptist.

"I know that. All I have to do is run faster than you!!" Well, so much for cooperation.

Hey, what do you do in those bad-to-worse case scenarios when you have to face a giant grizzly on your own? I'm referring to those imponderable, unforeseen circumstances that tend to blind-side us from time to time. Well, I don't know about you, but in those moments, I need to know that I am not alone. I need to know that I am part of a team that has genuine concern and care over its members. I need to know that if facing the angry grizzly of emotional /spiritual pain, personal loss or physical illness that I will not be abandoned.

As we examine our individual core values, it is very clear to me that concern for others is vital to mission accomplishment. In expressing this concern for people, we need to have an awareness of our surroundings, being ever vigilant of potential dangers and pit falls that could harm the other members of the team. I.e., I cover your back and you cover mine. I need to have your interest at heart because I will assume the same from you. Why? Because we are each valued members of the team and we need each other to accomplish our mission. That's the theory and when put into practice we find that the principles will actually work. This process attempts to ensure that we are not left alone in moments of difficulty (great or small).

However, in all our vigilance and proactive planning there is always room for a margin of error. There is always the possibility that in a given moment of personal difficulty I could find myself apparently alone. Well, even then, I still need to know that I am not alone. I need to know that I am inextricably connected and in fact am a part of the "City of God." In knowing this I am assured that while nations may be at war and kingdoms may rise and fall that at the end of the day God is still God. If I truly believe this (and I mean truly) I can be armed with the confidence of God's pre-eminent power and abiding presence. However, here is the caveat. I must be careful that my confidence is not an arrogant confidence. I must be careful not to fall into the trap of constantly asserting that God is on my side. Rather, I must ensure that I am on God's side.

Having to face the grisly from time to time may be a fact of life, but I do know that I am not alone. I have you, you have me and God has us.

⟐ *Devote yourselves to prayer, being watchful and thankful.*

*(Colossians 4:2)*

## PRAYER PLUS PENICILLIN

THE SCENE IS a doctor's office as the physician speaks to his patient: "Jim, you are in terrible shape! You simply have to do something about your condition. First, tell your wife to cook healthier meals. Then you have to stop working yourself to death. Work instead on creating a budget and stick to it. That will eliminate much stress. Make sure you take some time to relax. Unless you make those changes in your life, you'll probably be dead in thirty days!"

Jim's response: "Doc, it would sound more official coming from you. Would you mind calling my wife and sharing those instructions with her?"

While Jim made his way home, the doctor spoke with his wife on the phone and made her aware of the gravity of her husband's health condition. When Jim arrived home, his wife rushed up to him and said: "Honey, I just spoke with the doctor and I'm so sorry…. It sounds like you have thirty days to live." So much for empathy!

How we respond to the circumstances of life is a matter of choice. How life responds to us is quite beyond our control. Whenever you are looking for answers that lie beyond the doctor's prescription medication be assured that the power of a praying man/woman defies the circumstances of life. In fact, just pray. In times of trouble, pray. In times of joy, pray. In times of sickness, Pray!

I must humbly report to you that in spite of an advanced degree in theology and in spite of attending and teaching workshops and seminary courses on the dynamics and theology of prayer, I am yet to fully understand how prayer works. The more I try to dissect and analyze the depths of its reality the more I realize how superficial my understanding is. But I do know this… prayer works! I've seen it work in the life of people who "work it."

Please don't get me wrong. I am as much a believer in the marvels of modern medicine as the next person. You will see me running to the medicine cabinet and reaching for the aspirin at the slightest hint of a headache. Prayer and penicillin are not mutually exclusive. I vividly remember the day my three-year-old son underwent surgery. At the end of the operation, the attending surgeon met my wife and me in the waiting room and advised us to pray for the boy's recovery. I've been present at trauma centers when doctors have advised family members to pray because they had reached the limits of their medical skill.

The Medical Tribune (Volume 27, #1) related the story of Dr Randy Byrd, a San Francisco Cardiologist. Dr. Byrd is a former assistant professor of medicine at the University of California. The doctor is the author of a randomized study of 393 coronary care unit patients at San Francisco General Hospital. He arranged for prayer groups to pray for 192 of his patients, but not for 201 others. The results showed that those prayed for suffered fewer complications! Only three required antibiotics. Only 6 suffered pulmonary edema and none required intubations. Those for whom there was no prayer suffered more. Sixteen needed antibiotics. Eighteen suffered pulmonary edema. Twelve required intubations. The doctor's conclusion: "the patients who were prayed for did better."

You may call this a fluke. You may dismiss this as quackery. Nevertheless, you cannot dismiss the numerous other studies that affirm a link between prayer and well-being. The habitual presence of chaplains and chapels in practically all major hospitals attest to it.

I believe that prayer is the point where we can "touch" and discern the Almighty's direction. I believe that prayer is the place where we can get a taste of the pleasure of God. I believe that prayer is the platform where we can sense the power of God. If this is true, and I believe it is, it would follow that our own pleasure, comfort, purpose and inner power in life is directly related to our prayer life.

Nothing wrong with penicillin and there's nothing wrong with prayer.

# SECTION VI
## THE EMOTIONAL CYCLE

*And the peace of God, which transcends all under-standing, will guard your hearts and your minds in Christ Jesus.*

*(Philippians 4:7)*

### STRESSED TO THE MAX

ROGER MARIS IS a name familiar and sometimes revered by many baseball fans. It is recorded that in 1962 this gifted athlete broke the major league record for home runs in one season. What very few knew at the time was that because of the pressure to perform he suffered great anxiety. He even lost a lot of hair.

Late that season after having broken the record, Maris did a strange thing; he held up a game. He stepped back from home plate to watch a flock of geese pass over the right-field seats. This was unusual; a whole game, played before thousands of people stopped by one man who wanted to watch some geese!

Newly refreshed, Maris stepped back to the plate and hit the next pitch into the right-field seats just below the spot the geese had passed moments earlier. Years later when asked about the incident, Maris replied, "I can still see those geese. Watching them was so peaceful."

You don't have to be a highly paid and uniquely gifted sports star to feel the pinch of pressure that comes from a demanding career. You don't have to be famous to experience the stress that can be produced by tension-filled family responsibilities. You do not even have to be a top money earner to experience the stress induced by bad financial decisions. Sometimes you just simply need to find yourself in the wrong place and at the wrong time. You may not be looking for stressful experiences. Sometimes stress will find you instead. Let's face it. Stress is a part of life and we all start to experience it from the moment we come into the world.

Tension, stress, anxiety know no boundaries and are no respecters of status, position or authority. Stress is one of the great equalizers and does not discriminate. People at all levels of society and within all ranks of the military (chaplains not excluded) can experience moments of anxiety and distress produced by a whole myriad of factors, many of which are outside our direct control.

Like Roger Maris, people in turmoil still seek peace wherever and however they may find it. Unfortunately the search many times can lead one down misguided paths. The quick fix of alcohol and drugs might provide temporary peace or respite from the pressure to perform but in the long run intensify the pain that pressure can produce. The outcome produced by stressful lives can be negative, and sometimes leads to life-threatening suicidal thoughts if nothing is done to counteract its effects.

How can we deal with stress? What positive path can we take on the road to successfully addressing this problem? I offer the following for your consideration:

IDENTIFY IT: *This seems logical and almost appears ludicrous that I would bring this up. How can someone not know that he/she is experiencing stress? For many, "denial" of the problem becomes the common response. That is, putting up the "mask" that everything is fine but underneath it all, a volcano is preparing to erupt. When stress-filled, be quick to acknowledge it. Embrace its reality in your life and be prepared to share what you're feeling with those closest to you.*

SEEK HELP: *Stress can create the "tunnel vision" effect. It can cloud-over our thinking and prevent us from identifying positive alternatives. That is where the helpers can come in and help us identify healthy options. But we must be willing to talk! Close family and friends can be an immediate source of help. Do not hesitate to seek the help of mental health professionals. And, of course, chaplains and other clergy are always ready to provide unconditional support and counsel. As you share with those that desire to help you, you will become aware that others have successfully conquered this monster in the past. You will discover that you too can experience victory.*

ACT: *As those positive alternatives are identified, you are then called to ACT! Remember that as you act on those options, you will commence to assume a measure of control and personal responsibility. As you do so, you will become more confident in harnessing those factors that produced the stress to begin with. The long-term benefits are much too valuable to pass up. The promise of good health, overall happiness and contentment await those who take the initiative and …ACT!*

In closing, I must share with you a personal discovery that has represented an invaluable resource in fighting stress. You see, two thousand years ago an intellectual Hebrew man named Paul of Tarsus described a peace which had been revealed to him in the midst of his pressure and pain. He described it as a godly peace "which transcends all understanding which will guard your hearts and your minds…." This peace, which Paul referred to, is the peace that man should seek in times of stress. It is still available to all who seek it. Believe me; it is more peaceful than watching the geese pass over the right-field seats and more rewarding than hitting a home run.

⊹ *Even though I walk through the valley of the shadow of death, I will fear no evil, for you are with me; your rod and your staff, they comfort me.*
*(Psalm 23:4)*

## PEOPLE OF THE VALLEY

A MAN IN his elderly years was lying on his deathbed. He turned to his wife and said:

*"You know Gladys, you have always been with me through the good and bad times. Do you remember*

*the time I lost my job? You were right there by my
side. How about the time I had that terrible accident? You were right there to call the ambulance
when I fell off the roof and during those dark years
of the depression… when we had nothing… you were
there. During all those times, Gladys, you were right
there… in the valley of my despair. Now, here I am.
I'm lying here in terrible pain facing death's door. It
is the deepest valley experience of my life and you're
right here by my side as always. You know what
Gladys, YOU'RE BAD LUCK!"*

Well, the valley experiences in life can lead us to say and do
things that will reveal the true nature of our spirit. You may be very
familiar with "valley-type" experiences. You may be in the middle
of one right now. You may be trying to find your way out of the
valley and keep your faith intact in the process.

Gladys' husband had a humorous, though sad response to his
dilemma. In him, we find a man that allowed his valley experience
to look only for what or whom to lay the blame on. When it comes
to matters of life, death, sadness, loss, grief, or distress you can do
one of two things: you can lay the blame on others or you can lay
claim to God's manifold resources.

What is this "valley" thing anyway? Well, we might as well know
because we will find that much of living takes place in the valley.
In its most extreme form living in the valley involves the crisis of
loss, the humiliation of marital unfaithfulness, the frustration and
despair of addiction or even the pain of rebellious children. Otherwise, the valley is made up of the ordinary, mundane things of
day-to day living. That's where we have to prove our stamina and
strength.

Oh yes!.... Thank God for the occasional mountaintop experiences of life. We'll see the beautiful sunrises and the inspirational sunsets. We may even get a taste of the heavens, but shortly thereafter we return to the "valley."

Living in the valley becomes a test of our faith, of our character and our love for God. Living in the valley can make us better people or bitter people. We can become bitter if we jump to the wrong conclusions about why God has allowed a particular challenge to come along. We can become better if we open our eyes to God's power, wisdom, providence and everlasting love and mercy. Therefore dwelling in the valley appears to be divided between the victims and the victors. Which one are we?

If we're going to persevere and overcome we need to lay the blame game aside and learn the value and victory that comes from embracing the claims that God has on our lives. This is what is commonly known as "keeping the faith." It's the difference between being a victim or being a victor.

How then, do we keep the faith? DRAW NEAR TO GOD. Do so with the full assurance of your faith. All those who truly believe in God have access to God. In drawing near we do so sincerely, worshipfully and with an open heart as we seek God's wisdom.

Christian artist, Steve Green has a song about valley living:

"Hidden valleys produce a life song.

Hidden valleys will make a heart strong. Desperation can cause you to sing,

Hidden valleys turn shepherds to kings."

We find that great men and women of God have drawn near to God during their time in the valley. It is the place that God uses to shape his children.

✦ *But he said to me, "My grace is sufficient for you,
for my power is made perfect in weakness." Therefore I will boast all the more gladly about my
weaknesses, so that Christ's power may rest on me.*
(2 Corinthians 12:9)

## Down in the Dumps (on depression)

It is a condition most often associated with middle-aged men (ages 40-55). Some have called this experience the "mid-life crisis." However, it is no respecter of persons or age groups. It is not confined to particular genders and is not necessarily limited by age. It can be a time in anyone's life when one experiences the pain that comes along with unfulfilled dreams. Perhaps one feels forced to admit that he/she has only a limited amount of control over the conditions and circumstances that surround them. It is a time in life when reality denies and defies the ideals one had established.

The fact of the matter is that it is most simply defined as a bad bout of depression. The symptoms are a loss of hope, a low level of motivation, lack of energy and sometimes an exhausting battle of mental games. The inner struggle usually brings up a bunch of unanswered questions. The biggest question is typically: Why? The struggle with depression can bring about a dark and dismal personal disposition that can immobilize one mentally, emotionally and physically. In acute circumstances a person can even become physically ill. Whether for a moment, a month or years at a time, anyone of us can experience depression.

I am not a mental health specialist nor do I have advanced degrees in clinical counseling. I'm always to refer and access gifted clinical counselors that can provide invaluable support through the trying times posed by depression. By all means, we should use all the good resources made available to us. As a chaplain I seek to provide a faith-oriented option in confronting depression. When we cannot get the answers to the questions – when we cannot realize our goals – when the "real" destroys our "ideals" – when we ask in despair "where is God in all of this? " – When times are simply unjust…. You see, depression can destroy the myth of the old cliché "when things get tough the tough get going" because there are times, my friends, that there is no more toughness left! It is precisely in those moments that an unconditional, unadulterated faith in God must be exercised (along with other good resources).

Perhaps I can best relate this through a personal experience and what I learned from it. When our older son was four years old he underwent a series of elaborate surgeries. During that process I found myself gradually sinking into a depressive state. I sought help. A gifted hospital chaplain and the support and prayers of people that loved my family taught me a few things about exercising my faith in the midst of depression. I learned that:

GOD'S KNOWLEDGE IS COMPREHENSIVE: I believe in a sovereign God. I can try but I cannot fully discern the mind of God. I need to trust that God knows more than I do and I need to trade the facts of my existing situation for faith. It is an active faith which calls me to act upon those things over which I have some measure of control. Ultimately, my faith invites me to trust in the eternal knowledge and integrity of the divine and majestic being who is never surprised nor does he/she take naps. God's knowledge is comprehensive.

GOD'S TIME IS THE RIGHT TIME: God possesses the eternal calendar and God is always right on time. To put it in biblical terms: "In the fullness of time" God acts. God has dealt with his people.

The Almighty has intervened in history and still answers prayers. God has dealt with and wants to deal with me and with you. And, when the fullness of time comes…

GOD'S GRACE IS SUFFICIENT: I have learned that in the midst of personal anguish, grief, loss and depression God will use the circumstances to shape a person of faith. Much like the potter forms the clay God can and will use his grace to create a new work in our lives. The result can be a maturity born in strife and nurtured to strength by the hand of God.

> ⟨✝⟩ *But we ought always to thank God for you, brothers loved by the Lord, because from the beginning God chose you to be saved through the sanctifying work of the Spirit and through belief in the truth.*
> *(2 Thessalonians 2:13)*

## NO GUARANTEES

THE YOUNG HUSBAND got home all excited that day! "We've got a great insurance man, honey. He just sold me a policy that will pay you: $5,000 if I'm strangled, $10,000 if I die in a submarine and $200,000 if I die in an accident. Just think of how well-off we'll be if I'm accidentally strangled to death in a submarine!" The wife just stood there, totally speechless. The husband went on: "He also sold us a policy that will pay me $50.00 per week for life if I live longer than 90. That's so I won't be a burden on my mom and dad."

Insurance companies control vast amounts of investment capital. These firms have been successful in part because they thrive on two important psychological factors: our fears and our insecurities. President Roosevelt was once quoted as follows: "The only Dependable fortune teller that I have ever known is the life insurance man. He tells you what is going to happen and it does!" Don't get me wrong. I am grateful for good dependable insurance. My point is that in our uncertain times it is inescapable to assume the uncertainty of almost everything we're involved in: from the uncertainty of stock market investments, to the survivability of the social security system. We may have cause for concern regarding the not so fail-proof banking system to the invasive electronic computer virus. A good number of marriages opt for pre-nuptial agreements unsure about the strength of their marital vows. The planned obsolescence of products we buy motivates us to purchase extended warranties to protect our insecurity.

So, we strive to achieve a reasonable amount of security in this life. We want to be sure, from the insurance we buy to the deodorant we wear. Everybody wants to be sure. However, let's face it. Even in the security that we can afford to purchase, there will always be a measure of insecurity in the day-to-day matters of life regardless how much we try or how much capital we may control. Given this reality, each day becomes a brand new day. Let's face it. We don't know if in the twinkle of the eye we'll be here or departed from this life. However, there is good, in fact great news in the middle of all these uncertainties. You see, we do have some measure of control over the insecurities of life.

1.   WE CAN CONTROL OUR DECISIONS: While we cannot control many of the events and circumstances that life throws our way, we do have a measure of control as to how we decide to face life. Freedom from much anxiety and stress can become a reality when we choose how we will respond to circumstances.

2. WE CAN MANAGE OUR TIME: Each day we are granted a precious commodity called "time." This commodity is renewed each day. Once the "Time" is used (or misused) it cannot be recovered. The challenge for us is to decide how we will use our daily ration of 24 hours to its most productive. "Today I will act toward other people as though this might be my last day on earth. I will not wait for tomorrow. Tomorrow might not be there to use." (anonymous)

3. WE CAN MANAGE OUR RESOURCES: The word that comes to mind is stewardship. In days of antiquity the steward was granted full authority by the landlord to manage and make important decisions over the estate. In the same fashion, each of us have been granted stewardship over resources that we "cannot take with us." Think of our material resources as an estate that we borrowed to care for and hand over to the next generation.

4. WE CAN CHOOSE OUR FAITH: I have saved the best for last. For I am persuaded that what we ultimately believe in will drive all other choices we make in life.

*...But as for me and my household, we will serve the Lord.* (Joshua 24:15b)

> ⊹ *There is no fear in love. But perfect love drives out fear, because fear has to do with punishment. The one who fears is not made perfect in love.*
> *(1 John 4:18)*

## AN ANATOMY OF FEAR

IN MOMENTS OF fear the human body, through a series of complex psychological and neurological signals prepares itself for an emergency. The mind telegraphs various parts of the body to prepare to the fullest and the body mobilizes its resources. The breathing rate, the heartbeat, circulation and other physiological functions dramatically increase their activity.

The adrenal glands, located on top of the kidneys, secrete adrenalin hormones into the blood at an amazing rate. As it circulates throughout the body the adrenalin effects the 'fight or flight' reaction. The liver releases sugar into the blood to make more energy available for the brain and muscles. As the body diverts blood from the digestive system to the exterior muscles, the peristaltic movements of the stomach and intestines (those warm, comfortable ripples that move our food along during the relaxed state of the body) stop and thereby cause the butterfly feeling. The mouth may dry up, the hair may stand on end, and the hands may feel clammy. In order of their frequency, here are the top five symptoms: a pounding heart; muscular tension; dryness of mouth; perspiration; Butterflies in the stomach.

No, this article is not a lesson in physiology. Personally, I'd be too boring and misinformed as a teacher of physiology. The description we just read can be downloaded from any medical encyclopedia and it is a very revealing picture of the chemistry laboratory our bodies turn into when we are confronted with a fearful situation. To be sure, there are different levels of fear but even when it is passive fear our bodies start to react internally. Anne Landers, the syndicated newspaper advisor would receive an average of 10,000 letters per month from people burdened with some problem. She once observed that the one problem, which stood out above all others, seemed to be fear. Now, fear per se is not all bad. After all, God implanted this emotion in man and when fear is aroused and directed in the proper context it can help preserve life and limb. For example, fear of some imminent danger can save our life. Even stage fright, properly managed, is a source of energy. However, in its extreme form, fear can turn into a phobia and may have to be treated as we might treat an illness. Thank God that most of us will never get to that extreme. For the most part, we will deal with the more mundane version such as fear of losing our job or maybe fear of aging. Fear of economic downturns or fear that our kids will get into trouble can also be part of our plight. Maybe fear of an IRS audit can get some people upset. The list of common fears can get exhaustive and if taken collectively can make us lose a few heartbeats. As we examine the anatomy of fear we can learn a few things about confronting fear and overcoming it.

First, we must identify our fear(s). Right now, this instance, answer this question: "What exactly is it that I'm afraid of?" Get right down real and identify the source of some particular personal fear. Second, be prepared to discuss your fear. Seek the counsel of the wise. It is amazing how much pressure is taken off when we are willing to verbalize our fear. The success of support groups across the nation is primarily due to people willing to discuss their fear(s). People experience a sense of healing in doing so as God uses others to offer encouragement and strength. Third, be prepared to act on your fear. You see, fear has a tendency to grow and can create irrational reactions on our part. We can cut fear down to size when we decide to "act on it." I suggest that we can act on our fear when we move closer to God who is the source of all courage. If we just concentrate on our fear we will tend to move away from God. We overcome our fear by trusting in God's power to give us personal serenity. To be sure, I haven't overcome all of my fears but God is not finished with me yet.

⊹ *To him who overcomes, I will give the right to sit with me on my throne, just as I overcame and sat down with my Father on his throne.*
*(Revelation 3:21)*

## I FALL DOWN. I GET UP

A WISE CHAPLAIN once said "The three hardest things to do in all the world are: to climb a wall that is leaning towards you, to kiss a girl that is leaning away from you and to be a chaplain with a simple message (not necessarily in that order). Well, I have never tried to climb a wall leaning towards me…but… I do have some experience in trying…to be a chaplain with a simple message. Sometimes I speculate if climbing the slanted wall or kissing the leaning girl may be easier. The difficulty of the "simple message" is in trying to get people to understand the simplicity of a very profound and potentially life-changing message. The key word here is simplicity. It is a message that tells people that they can be lifted up from the blight of a purpose- less life. It is a message that simply tells people that if you have fallen, you can get up.

In the mid 1990's there appeared a television commercial that featured an elderly lady who had fallen down in her house. She became immobilized. While sprawled-out on the floor she reaches for a device, a call button, hanging from her neck. She pushes the button and speaks into the device saying: "I've fallen, and I can't get up." Some people thought the commercial was comical due to the lady's shrill voice and exaggerated gestures. However, I remember having feelings of sadness when I saw the commercial. After all, here was a lonely, panic-stricken senior citizen, who had to depend on machinery. But it was sad for one other reason. It was sad because it is symbolic of many people (perhaps some of us) who have fallen into the deception of thinking that when we can't get up. You know what I mean. Perhaps it was an indiscreet decision that got you involved in the wrong relationship and what happened should have never happened. Possibly you said or did something that has deeply offended. You may have allowed some old negative behaviors to once again dominate some area of your life. It is also possible that you may have been at the receiving end of someone's abusive behavior. These different things can and will take their toll on your psyche and emotions. Consequently, you may be carrying this huge, burlap bag full of guilt, resentment or regret, which is weighing you down. You feel that you have fallen and that you cannot get up.

Well, here is the simple message: you have fallen, and you can get up! What makes it so difficult to communicate this? Well, people are looking for complicated solutions to their dilemmas. To be sure, there are complicated problems that can develop in life that may require hard work to fix. But the simple, bottom-line reality is that God is bigger than any problem that we may face this side of heaven and the power of God can set us back on our feet and restore us if we would simply surrender in faith to God's eternal source of grace and love for us.

How do I know this? Well, my book of faith teaches me that "... God so loved the world that he gave...." I have learned and continue to be reminded that at the very center of God's heart is God's love for humanity. If God's love for his creation is so all encompassing, then it follows that if I fall I can get up because I have been created for good purpose.

So, exactly how can we go about "getting up?" Here are two suggestions that, faithfully applied, can make a great deal of difference.

1. Apologize whenever necessary: In the foreword to the wonderfully practical book, The One Minute Apology the authors state: "Few things are more powerful than having the common sense, wisdom, and strength to admit when you've made a mistake and to set things right." Indeed, it is amazing what can happen when we are quick to apologize in those moments of personal fault

2. Forgive and let go: "Bitterness is a poison that you swallow and hope that the other person will die." I love this quote! I don't know who said it but whoever did deserves a medal. A component of forgiveness is letting go of our demand for revenge and allowing God to restore us and exact his judgment on the unrepentant.

꜔ *I have told you these things, so that in me you may have peace. In this world you will have trouble. But take heart! I have overcome the world.*
*(John 16:33)*

## WHY NOT ME?

DR. LEON TUCKER, a gifted preacher and teacher once told the account of a woman who had been emotionally broken by a great tragedy in her life. She had been living under the crushing weight of her pain for so long that her faith and fervent devotion to God had given way to constant resentment and complaint. One day she finally cried out from the bitterness of her soul: "O God I wish I had never been born!" Such was the bitterness of her spirit.

In response to her words of despair, a friend who was present wisely responded, "why, my dear child, you are not fully made yet; you are only being made, and you are quarreling with God's process."

You ever have one of those days when the crushing weight of your emotional pain pressed down on your shoulders? Ever have one of those days when you've given people the best you have and have received in turn nothing but criticism and complaint? It's on these kinds of days when in total despair we may turn to God and ask, "Have You brought me this far just for this?"

In times of antiquity, there was a place in the Sinai Desert known as the "Wilderness of Shur." A small oasis could be found there which was named The Waters of Marah (Hebrew for bitterness). It was named "Marah" to remind a people of the bitterness produced by trying times. It was a time in the history of Israel when the people of "The Book" had toiled with bitterness and discontent.

None of us are exempt from those times. Indeed, we can quickly find ourselves going from moments of triumph to times of trouble and personal testing. The "waters of discontent" can occur at anytime in our lives or in the lives of those we love.

In his classic work "The Problem of Pain" C. S. Lewis wrote: "God whispers to us in our pleasures, speaks in our conscience, but shouts in our pains: It is God's megaphone to rouse a deaf world" (Collier Books, NY, 1962).

Our "waters of discontent" is a place of circumstance, events or experiences in the journey of life. It may be the bitter realization of an illness or that difficult situation with your child or other important relationship.

When we arrive at our "waters of discontent" our question should not be, "why me?" Rather, our question should be, "why not me?" Please be assured that in those times of trial God draws near to us and makes a statement. The Almighty will turn a time of testing into a time of teaching.

You see, I believe that God uses the circumstances of life to further shape our personality. The Almighty can use our painful experiences to help us understand our utter and total dependence on the Divine.

But all this begs the question. For if God is all-powerful and if God is not the author of evil then why does God allow evil? Why do God's Children suffer? Why do bad things happen to good people? Well, the fact of the matter is that everybody suffers. The good as well as the bad suffer because the world is inherently imperfect. Amid our God-given freedom and innate imperfection wrong decisions are made and lessons are learned. It is in the learning where God can do a great work in our lives, if we are open to it.

The point here is that whether we have been lead into the "waters of discontent" or have stumbled into it, God will meet us there! It is at that point that we are individually faced with a decision. We must decide whether God is truly Lord of our life or not. We must then decide whether we will allow God to heal our bitterness or not. It becomes a decision of transcendent proportions with equally transcendent possibilities.

⸙ *I waited patiently for the LORD; he turned to me and heard my cry. He lifted me out of the slimy pit, out of the mud and mire; he set my feet on a rock and gave me a firm place to stand.*

*(Psalm 40:1-2)*

## PARADIGM SHIFT

I GUESS THERE are few things in life that are more miserable than being severely sea-sick on the high seas without any possibility of relief. Thankfully, the good Lord has blessed me with good sea legs, but I have witnessed first hand the experience of those without any hope of relief.

There is the account of one poor soul traversing a rough ocean passage. The vessel was not totally sea-worthy and was being tossed around in tumultuous seas. The man became very seasick. He became claustrophobic and struggled topside and positioned himself on the rail of the ship. He held on to the rail and in the process he "lost" everything else (if you know what I mean). A sailor walked by and comforted him. "Sir, I know this seems bad for the moment but trust me. No one has ever died of seasickness." With all the strength the man could muster, he straightened himself out. He turned his "green" face to the sailor and said, "Son, don't tell me that. It's only the wonderful prospect of dying that keeps me alive."

Although I've never been seasick, I think I know how he must have felt. There have been times in my emotional life that have mirrored the experience. Thank God, it is not very often but sometimes we get caught in the "muck and mire" of life. We may get caught-up in the rut of repetitive, negative events that appear to have no end in sight. The issues of life will toss us in the sea of uncertainty and take us to those desolate places of existence where the thought may cross our minds: "Lord, go ahead and punch my card. I'm ready to go home. Take me out." It is the terrible experience of feeling stuck spiritually and emotionally. Feelings of nausea and depression could very well accompany this experience. When we arrive at those places in life it is OK to admit it. It is an arena of life that we may have to do battle in.

Finding ourselves in a rut and bogged down in the muck and mire (definition: soft, moist barnyard manure) of life can happen at any time. Losing our momentum our vision and our hope can happen to the sharpest and brightest among us. In those tender moments we may start to ask some ultimate questions such as: "God, Why…? Where are you?" "What am I doing here?" "Why are things not progressing at the rate I desire?"

Well, here are some suggestions that have helped me in past experiences:

1. BE PATIENT: These are words I love to hate because instant gratification is the motto of our times. When our vehicle gets stuck in the mud the natural inclination is to step on the gas thinking that it will work, right? Wrong! Stepping on the gas will bury us even deeper. The solution is to get out of the car, put traction under the tire and slowly, methodically tap the accelerator. In much the same way, when life seems out of control, take pause and "chill out." Look ahead with eager and confident expectation as we fix our eyes on God. Develop a personal disposition of dependency on God and then move ahead to…

2. CHANGE NEGATIVE HABITS: Arriving at the muck and mire of life is a gradual process. It takes place slowly as we start to gradually slip. Maybe we made a little compromise here and there. Eventually we find ourselves bogged down in some vicious negative cycle. Making corrections and adjustments in deficient areas takes personal initiative and courage. Changing negative habits requires a

daily decision of our will as we daily decide to get back to the basics of good and practical habits that affirm our moral, spiritual and ethical convictions

3. STAY ACCOUNTABLE: Identify an inner circle of wise and mature individuals that can be trusted for advice and confidentiality. These are people that we can share our feelings and concerns with and will honestly share their insights and help us to identify positive options. Staying accountable with them will keep us consistent.

4. DRAW NEAR TO GOD: Some of us expect very little from God. If we expected nothing, then we will look for nothing. Let us be assured that God is waiting to respond to us as we develop a disposition of dependency upon God.

✢ *Therefore I tell you, do not worry about your life, what you will eat or drink; or about your body, what you will wear. Is not life more important than food, and the body more important than clothes?*

*(Matthew 6:25)*

## DON'T WORRY, BE HAPPY!

"Here's a little song I wrote
Might want to sing it note for note,
Don't worry.... Be happy !"

IT WAS A catchy little ditty that became popular in the early 1990's. A music video was produced featuring the singer casually lounging on his hammock in the tranquil surroundings of his Caribbean island paradise. Well, the song had a definite appeal, but it wasn't always real because worrying, sooner or later is a very real part of our existence. In fact, it bothers me when people approach me and say those words: "don't worry." Doesn't it bother you? What do they mean by "don't worry"? After all no one is walking in my shoes. I'm the one paying the bills at the end of the month and I'm responsible for putting food on the table.

Can you identify with any of the following Olympic-type record holders on worry? There's the chronic worrier who joined the local chapter of the Don't Worry Club only to express helplessly: "Now I hold my breath. I'm so afraid I'll worry that I'm almost worried to death!" How about the patient who goes to his therapist and the counselor says: "Most things you worry about don't happen." "I know that. But then I find myself worrying about why they don't happen!!" Finally there's the worried young man whose fortune-teller says to him, "you'll be poor and unhappy until you are thirty." "And then what?" he asked. "Then you'll get used to it," she said. We may resemble some of these scenarios. They may echo some of our attitudes.

We may even laugh at ourselves for unnecessary worrying, and we're allowed to laugh at ourselves. But, on closer analysis worrying will debilitate us. It can and will drain us of our energy and chronic worrying can induce a serious threat to our health. What does worry do after all. Will worrying eliminate the problems? Will worrying place in my hands the key to the solutions? My experience is that worrying doesn't solve problems – rather it tends to compound the problems.

It's interesting to note that in classical Greek the word "worry" meant, "to divide the mind." Worrying will do that. It will divide and distort our thinking and "a divided mind is unstable in all ways" (James 1:8) Worrying will divide our energies so that we are drawn away from possible solutions. Ultimately, worrying becomes irrelevant because it does not change things. It really doesn't help in effectively coping with problems. Besides burning-up valuable energy it will also not add to our life span and may even limit the days of our life through stress related illnesses.

Freedom from worry does not demand that we negate all materialism and crawl into a cave to live like a hermit. Rather, freedom from worrying calls us to positive action as a lifestyle. We are challenged to free ourselves today from the unnecessary anxiety that comes from not knowing the problems of tomorrow. These unknown problems of the future are for the most part totally out of our control.

Freedom from worry calls us to responsible planning using the resources we have available today. To be sure, reasonable goal setting and planning will eliminate most worrying. With good planning we will learn the art of living in a day-tight compartment. We will enjoy the blessings of the present moment with a hopeful and purposeful look towards tomorrow.

A colleague and good friend put it this way in one of his sermons:
"When I work, I work hard.
When I sit, I sit easy.
And when I worry...I go to sleep!

# SECTION VII
## THE ART OF LIVING

*✛ The thief comes only to steal and kill and destroy;
I have come that they may have life and have it
to the full.*

*(John 10:10)*

### THE INCREDIBLE EXPERIENCE OF BEING

THE DOCTOR HAD some bad news and good news for his patient. "Sam" the doctor said. "You have a serious ailment. You need an operation right away." Well, Sam got a bit pale. He turned to his doctor and asked, "Is it that serious?" "Yes," said the doc. "Five out of six who undergo this operation die. But you have nothing to worry about." "Why not doctor?" asked Sam. "Well Sam, my last five patients have died. So, I know you're going to make it."

Well, I don't know what level of reassurance that gave to the patient, but I think you'll agree that when it comes to matters of life and death we know we are dealing with serious business. Regardless of how we may try to make light of it through humorous anecdotes, the serious matter of life and death (and in some cases life or death) is sure to catch our attention. Life and death address existence itself. To be or not to be is an issue of ultimate importance. There are no subtle definitions involved. You don't have to worry about what the definition of "is" is, that is, you either are or are not. "Whatever is, is." There is no statement in secular life worthier of contemplation.

We can hardly make a sentence in the English language without using some form of the verb "to be." The idea of "being" itself is filled with significance and potential. This is because having "being" means that we have the ability to reason, to think and solve problems. We are also relational in our being, having the ability to give and receive real love. In addition, we possess a moral consciousness, giving us the ability to discern right from wrong.

My faith teaches me that I possess these qualities because I've been created in the likeness of The Creator. What it all boils down to is that you and I have purpose! Having purpose should compel us to strive for the very best our abilities have to offer.

Matters related to existence, survival and preservation of life have been central to humanity since pre-historic times. In the past months and years "life or death" has been part of the national reality as we've engaged in a war that has resulted in the death of many and the grief of many more. Our political and military leaders have struggled with decisions that would directly impact matters of life and death. Their struggle is founded on the truth that life is precious; Life is irreplaceable; life is a responsibility. Therefore, …

1. HANDLE WITH CARE: We are surrounded by the marvels of modern technology. No other era in history has possessed the scientific means for the preservation and duration of life. As a society we acknowledge the importance of life and use our technology to prolong it. Ironically, however, that

same technology has been used to undermine and destroy life. We are also plagued by addictive lifestyles and destructive behaviors totally unprecedented. "Life is precious. Handle with care!"

2. LIVE IT ABUNDANTLY: Abundant living means responsible living. Given the number of choices we face daily, we are called upon to exercise our choices in a responsible and moral manner. Abundant living is balanced living in which we enjoy the good and pleasant things of life in a balanced, non-excessive way.

3. SHARE "LIFE" WITH OTHERS: "It is better to give than to receive." This old adage can be a driving force in reshaping the world. Think about this. Our country's population makes up approximately five percent of the world's population and yet we consume more than forty percent of the world's resources. The potential for improving the plight of the less fortunate is tremendous through a more equitable distribution of the world's resources. Sharing with others starts with the individual as each of us decides to bless another's life.

"So live that after the minister has ended his remarks, those present will not think they have attended the wrong funeral." (Anonymous)

✦ *...be prepared in season and out of season; correct, rebuke and encourage—with great patience and careful instruction.*

*(2 Timothy 4:2)*

## BE PREPARED

A MINISTER, ALREADY having preached about an hour, noticed one of his church members sleeping. Embarrassed, the minister motioned for an usher. The usher located the sleeping man and, taking a long stick, gently tapped him. The man snored on. The usher tapped him again, but a little firmer. The man continued to enjoy his sweet dreams.

By this time the usher's face was red with embarrassment, and it was then that the usher soundly whacked the man's head. The man slumped from the pew and fell on the floor. Thinking he had really injured the man, the usher knelt at his side only to hear him mutter, "Hit me again. I can still hear him."

Being prepared for all contingencies is not an easy thing, especially when it comes to listening to long-winded preachers or boring chaplain's articles. But, being prepared is a must in my world. So, if you fall asleep while reading this article be prepared for the "long stick."

I was a Boy Scout as a child. Some of my fondest childhood memories come from that period in my life. I liked being a Scout so much that I literally had to be asked to leave when I became too old for it. I remember the motto of Scouting: *Be Prepared*. I remember the tremendous amount of preparation and attention to detail that went into every camping trip. Our Troop (729) is located in New York City and we were real purists. We slept in tents in all kinds of weather. Ten and eleven-year old boys hiked for miles with forty to fifty pounds on our backs. We were taught to survive each experience. We were also prepared to help each other. These memories are still very much alive in me today along with the motto, *Be Prepared*.

The motto implied that we were to be prepared at all moments. But you know, it never occurred to me to ask: "Prepared for what?"

I just accepted on faith that I had to be prepared. In scouting the motto became an integral part of a belief system, which hopefully translated itself into practical daily living.

Many years later I came to better appreciate that "being prepared" is primarily an attitude, a life style, if you will. As a boy I didn't fully understand the long-term value of that principle which still resonates in me today. Many years later I also came to understand that the Boy Scouts had not invented the motto. It was actually borrowed. Deep in the pages of my Bible I read "Be prepared, in season and out of season."

Being prepared is pretty all encompassing. The challenge of the call demands attention to all facets of life. Being prepared has a special meaning to all of us who regularly are required to do things beyond our natural desires and abilities. There are five priorities that are given the highest place for those of us who strive to be prepared.

1. BE PREPARED to stand for the truth: We are to be first, last and always to be proclaimers of truth. Be it in reporting to our superiors or in a casual conversation in a restaurant..
2. BE PREPARED in season and out of season. That is, be instant; be urgent today not tomorrow because we don't know what tomorrow brings. The opportunities that appear today will quickly vanish at the dawn of a new day.
3. BE PREPARED to correct those that are heading in the wrong direction. Intervene in the lives of those that desperately need help but are afraid to ask.
4. BE PREPARED to rebuke with love and careful concern those that insist on making decisions and

taking actions that pose a detriment to themselves and others.

5. BE PREPARED to encourage and instruct those that are placed under our supervision. The power of positive mentoring must never be underestimated.

*⊕* *Do not conform any longer to the pattern of this world, but be transformed by the renewing of your mind.*

*(Romans 12:2)*

## "GIGO"

THE DARING EXPLOITS of our courageous astronauts of the 1960's is the stuff of which legends are made. Not only did they have "the right stuff," but they also had the right equipment and data support that made ultimate success possible. As you know computers were essential to the success and ultimate survival of our astronauts. A little ingenuity and sporadic flashes of intuition were also key elements

Whether you have seen the movie, you may be familiar with the near fatal mission of Apollo 13. This mission was nearly aborted because the spaceship became crippled in space. The story goes that a computer spent 84 minutes discovering and correcting the problem of how to get the crew safely back to earth. What the computer calculated in 84 minutes, would have taken a man with pencil and paper many years to solve. Such were the difficulties of the calculations.

Overall, computers and the information they process have become an indispensable part of life. The quality of the information computers provide must be reliable, accurate and many times indisputable. The extent of a computer's dependability will either be enhanced or hindered by the quality of the data that is inputted into its memory. If you feed it garbage, it will give you garbage. Therefore, Garbage In, Garbage Out (GIGO... get it?). GIGO is the acronym used to describe a computer that is turning out bad or misleading information. That is, someone fed bad data (garbage) into its memory and consequently the machine feeds back inaccurate information (garbage). Well, enough of this garbage. I think you get the picture.

Like computers, we all need reliable data for determining good direction. Long before computers were common to our culture, humanity was "designed" to receive good data that would then create the output for abundantly good and healthy lives. Please note that the basic design is still there. We continue to long in our hearts to receive and know the truth. In each one of us lays the choice for deciding the quality of the data that will "program" our lifestyle, morals and sense of spirituality. As we choose good, sound data we will be able to fulfill the functions for which we were created. We will live with a sense of purpose.

Now, when that purpose goes unfulfilled, there is a malfunction. We will start to experience the GIGO effect. Computers can malfunction and so can we. Are you with me so far? Like computers, we will only be as smart and as effective as the program or data I choose to input. However, the difference between a computer and us is one of choice. We possess the privilege of picking our program, our data source. The data we choose will become the source for proper decision-making. Choosing good, reliable data is a continuous process in life.

Well, here is my suggestion. If the all-knowing God, the source of all the data in the entire universal computer bank, can become our personal data source, then the human spirit will have an enormous capacity for brilliance. God's input will "stay put." I will have data that possesses eternal and positive consequences.

INPUT! INPUT! We all need good input. Without good input there is bad output (GIGO).

⊹ *Without the assistance of the Divine Being ... I cannot succeed. With that assistance, I cannot fail.*
(Abraham Lincoln)

⊹ *...and your life is now hidden with Christ in God.*
(Colossians 3:3)

## "...Can Someone Tell me who I am?"

ON THE LIGHTER side ... a very upset wife visited the family psychiatrist and said to him, "Doctor, you've got to help my husband. He's having delusions and thinks he's an elevator." "Oh ...you just send him to see me. I'll straighten him out," said the psychiatrist. "I can't do that," said the wife. "He's an express and doesn't stop on your floor." (Laugh, please)

On the darker side, however... is a true story from the annals of World War I. The story goes that at the conclusion of "the war to end all wars" numerous shell-shocked French soldiers could not remember who they were. They were the survivors of massive artillery barrages. Literally, hundreds of shells had exploded around them but they had been miraculously spared. However, mentally they were scarred. The soldiers were disoriented to the point of not knowing who they were. Try to imagine, if you can, the confusion, the horror, the anxiety of not having any blessed idea of who you are! These French soldiers had a true identity crisis.

A number of them could not be reunited with family due to faulty military records. For these poor souls the question of the moment was: "Please, please... can someone tell me who I am?"

Who are you? Who am I? The question appears, trite, almost ridiculous. But, at the heart of the question lies the all-important issue of "self identity." The answer to the question must go beyond merely describing what we do for a living or what our physical appearance may be like. Immeasurably more important than our professional identity is... our spiritual and moral identity. These non-tangible qualities of the self ultimately define who we are.

When it comes to grinding out the practical aspects of daily living, having a clear and healthy self-identity will keep us balanced, consistent, and happy with life. We will do what we say and say what we do. Let me illustrate:

A farmer was on his way to New Orleans with a big Bible tucked under his arm. A friend stopped him and asked where he was going. The farmer answered that he was on his way to Mardi Gras to indulge in wine, women and whatever else came along. Puzzled by the reply, the friend asked why he was taking his Bible. The farmer replied: "Well, if I stay over the weekend I want to make sure I get to church." The farmer had projected some mixed signals. His inner motives betrayed his outer appearance.

Can we talk? Let's face it. As we look across the landscape of life, I think that we can agree that the three traps of the soul are: money, sex, power. These are the three general excesses that commonly entrap people in a negative downward spiral.

It appears crystal clear to me that in our personal spiritual and moral identity there are certain things that do not fit, that must not be allowed to distort and undermine a healthy self-identity. There are things that are appropriate and things that are not.

Is this easy to do? No. It takes work and sometimes the work is uphill. Famous scholar and author, C.S. Lewis expressed it this way: "anyone that has ever said that it's easy to be good has never tried to be good." The stakes are high when we hold up the standard for that which is good and right. In doing so we may get bloody, we may even get hurt. However, the positive end-results and benefits to others and us are immeasurable.

When our self-identity is anchored and centered on the things of God we will discover great personal comfort, internally and externally.

> ⊹ *Even the sparrow has found a home, and the swallow a nest for herself, where she may have her young—a place near your altar, O LORD Almighty, my King and my God.*
>
> *(Psalm 84:3)*

## THE GREAT HOMECOMING

AN IDAHO MAN went fishing at Lake Crescent, leaving his very pregnant wife at home. She was in her ninth month. As far as fishing trips go, it was a big success. He caught the biggest trout ever. The man was absolutely elated! He was so crazy with joy the he emailed his wife: "I've got one; weighs 7 pounds and is a beauty."

Shortly Following, he got a reply from his wife: "So have I; weighs 8 pounds 4 ounces. Not a beauty, looks like you. COME HOME!"

We all need to hear those magical words: "Come Home." It is good to know that good looks do not qualify us for coming home. It is also good to know that even after dismally failing at fishing, we can still come home. But, what does coming home mean?

We typically define the home as the physical structure. Perhaps home is the place where we were raised, that is, a geographical location. I submit to you that that is not your home. The physical structure is a house (not a home). The boundaries of its physical and geographical location are simply a dot on a map. Moreover, let's face it, the house and location where we were raised may not necessarily inspire the warmest of memories. To "come home" is a lot more than that.

"Coming home" says everything that ever needs to be said. "Coming home" says everything that man ever needs to hear. Home is where we find peace. Home is where we find safety, forgiveness and acceptance. It is a place of safety and stability in the midst of turmoil. Home is where we come to terms with life. Home is where the heart is! (I Couldn't resist that one.)

Indeed, there was a time in my life that I desperately needed to get that message: "Come Home." When I did, I found peace. Periodically I still need to hear that message: "Come Home." It happens when I allow the non-essential issues of life to take center stage and I start to "major on the minors." My spirit becomes embroiled with petty issues. My ego and pride get in the way of things and I can't find inner peace. In those moments the "come home" invitation is like music to my ears. When I come home I reassert my purpose and reasons for living. When I come home I realize that it is not all about me but that it is all about God and those people that surround and touch my life with love, encouragement and support. The family and friends that surround my life are seen as precious gifts from God. These are the people that help me to feel vibrantly alive when I "come home." When I "come home" I can better cope with the realities of life in all of its diversity.

The story is told of a little girl who received a toy poodle named "Happy" for her birthday. Well, Happy wasn't too happy when he arrived at his new home. The little girl built him an oversized doghouse. Happy didn't like it. Even food and water would not lure him into it. One day the little girl climbed into the doghouse and the dog followed. It was a new day for Happy! The fears were gone. The loneliness was dispelled. The puppy came to know his owner and found a place of safety, trust and peace. Happy had come home!

When we come home we can experience the fullness of life. It can become life's answers to all those who have spent their lives casting their fishing lines on the wrong side of the boat.

So, in closing, I hope we have caught or perhaps recaptured the meaning of coming home! The pay-off in "coming home" is in savoring the Almighty's love and blessings through healthy relationships, growth experiences and an inner peace that transcends all understanding.

⊹ *And we know that in all things God works for the good of those who love him, who have been called according to his purpose.*

*(Romans 8:28)*

146

## What's your Purpose?

Who's asking that question anymore? Who's asking about purpose and value in life? Well, I'm of the opinion that everyone really wants to know their purpose, their proper function and their value. I know that because of what I do for a living. After counseling with enough people who are trying to define and understand their purpose I am persuaded to believe that we all need to identify our reason for living.

Why am I here? What is the plan? What drives your life? These are equally compelling questions that beg for an answer. To be sure, whatever drives you will define your purpose. Identifying that purpose will define your direction and give shape to your character (or lack there of). That's how important defining your purpose is! If we can acknowledge that purpose and embrace it, a completely new world of possibilities opens-up. In defining our purpose we can commence to live significantly. Life is then lived based on personal convictions, always striving to effect positive change. Four words define the contours of purpose:

1. PEOPLE: Life (this side of heaven) is about people! We can't get away from that. A great part of our purpose is found in relationship to others. Life is about people because the creation of humanity was God's crowning achievement. Dr. Martin Luther King well expressed it: "Life's persistent and most urgent question is: what are you doing for others?"

2. PRIORITY: A purpose will give you the proper priorities. Priorities will simplify life by eliminating whatever is superfluous and thereby reduce

frustration. If your priorities are in proper balance you'll know your business. Priorities, which are recognized and properly arranged, will give you the ability to say "NO" to whatever doesn't fulfill your purpose.

3. PASSION: If you possess purpose then you will have passion for your life's work, and vision. That passion will come from your convictions and will motivate you to be your best self in all circumstances. The challenge is to maintain your commitment and your passion as consistently as possible.

4. POWER: Power for living is not generated by physical characteristics. It has nothing to do with physical stamina but everything to do with spiritual strength. It is intangible and difficult to measure. However, it is absolutely essential as we strive to maintain our focus on our priorities and passion for living; I believe that the power of our spirit is correlated to our relationship with the living God. It is this special power of the spirit that will not allow us to give up when all else seems lost.

In his incomparable work Robert Fulghum points out a startling reality as follows: *"The statisticians figure that about 60 billion people have been born so far. And as I said, there's no telling how many more there will be, but it looks like a lot. And yet-and here comes the statistic of statistics-with all the possibilities for variation among the sex cells produced by each person's parents, it seems quite certain that each one of the billions of human beings who has ever existed has been distinctly different from every other human being, and that this will continue for the indefinite future.*

*In other words, if you were to line up on one side of the earth every human being who ever lived or ever will live, and you took a good look at the whole motley crowd, you wouldn't find anybody quite like you."* (All I Really Need to Know I Learned in Kindergarten, 1988 Random House, Inc.)

Moral of the story? You are unique! You have purpose! Let's get to work!

<blockquote>

✢ *You, my brothers, were called to be free. But do not use your freedom to indulge the sinful nature; rather, serve one another in love.*

*(Galatians 5:13)*

</blockquote>

## PLEASURE MATTERS

HER HUSBAND WAS a golfing extremist... "Fanatic" better described him. She was a weekend golf widow. One morning at the breakfast table she just let out her feelings: I'm sick and tired of being left alone every weekend! If you think you're going to play golf today you've got another thing coming. And, if you play today you'll find your bags packed and waiting for you." "Oh nonsense," replied the husband, as he reached for the toast. "Golf is the farthest thing from my mind. Now, would you pass me the nine iron- I mean the butter?"

What is it about pleasure that can drive us to extremes? Some of us can become immersed in the pleasures of personal hobbies. Our hobbies can become addictive to the exclusion of other very important things. In fact, anyone of us can become totally absorbed in pleasures to the negation of our own humanity. Such is the influence that personal pleasures can sway over us.

Epicurus was a Greek philosopher who lived 300 BCE He taught that nothing exists but atoms and space. These atoms are always in the process of forming new combinations or new matter. Epicurus maintained that when a person dies his personality reverts back to atoms and goes on to form new combinations. Therefore, he believed, that matter is all that exists and that this life is all that counts. Consequently, man needs to make pleasure and happiness his chief aim in life. Humanity's chief aim should be to avoid pain and indulge in as many pleasures as possible. "Drink and be merry, for tomorrow we die." If death ended it all, why not indulge the flesh. Indeed, Epicurus can be identified as the first true hedonist.

Hey, what do you take personal pleasure in? Does pleasure matter to you? It should. Should a responsible person indulge in pleasurable experiences? Certainly. The preamble to our declaration of Independence, framed by responsible, God-fearing individuals, states that we have been endowed by the creator with life, liberty and the "pursuit of happiness." How we individually interpret "happiness" or the pursuit of pleasure will greatly determine the extent to which priorities are made.

It doesn't take much of an astute observer to notice the effects of over-indulgence in our society. In many instances what constitutes a proper definition and application of pursuing happiness seems to have run-amok. Is there a balance? Yes! Can one be responsible and experience pleasure in life? Absolutely! To be sure, experiencing happiness and the pleasures of this life are totally compatible with the good life that the Creator has given to us.

Our freedom in experiencing the pleasures of life must be seen in the light of responsible restraint, sensitivity to the needs of others and a sense of shared accountability. This means that in my pursuit of pleasures I am accountable to you as you are accountable to me. This needs to happen within an atmosphere of mutual consideration and respect. Therefore, I am not free to do whatever will give me pleasure. We must all examine our individual pursuit of pleasure within the parameters of personal relationships. I submit the following questions to consider in making decisions regarding pleasurable pursuits:

- WILL MY DECISION IN ANY WAY SPECIFICALLY VIOLATE GOD'S INTENDED GUIDELINES FOR MY LIFE? The answer to this question is either Yes or No. The 10 commandments is a good place to start. These commandments are universal in scope and form the basis of western jurisprudence.

- WILL THIS PLEASURE HURT ME IN ANY WAY? Consider the short and long-term effects.

- HOW WILL MY DECISION IMPACT MY NEIGHBOR?

- HOW WILL MY DECISION GLORIFY GOD?

In closing ...*do what leads to peace and to mutual edification.* (Romans 14:19)

⊹ *He redeemed us in order that the blessing given to Abraham might come to the Gentiles through*

*Christ Jesus, so that by faith we might receive the*
*promise of the Spirit.*

*(Galatians 3:14)*

## In Memory of a Promise Kept

"I SHALL RETURN!" These words had a prophetic ring when spoken by General Douglas MacArthur on 11 March 1942. The set of circumstances, which surrounded the General's remark, were at best hopeless.

Those were difficult days for America. You see, the Japanese Imperial Army had successfully invaded the Philippines. World War II was raging in the Pacific and the U.S. mainland was threatened with invasion or direct attack. General MacArthur, one of our premiere military minds, was in danger of being captured by the Japanese. Consequently, President Roosevelt ordered him to abandon the Philippines. The General reluctantly obeyed.

Indeed, few of us can appreciate those dark moments. For those who lived through those days "I shall return" had a special appeal. The words were uttered with conviction. The words were filled with certainty. The brevity of its message underlined the clarity and commitment of the speaker. There was no question in anybody's mind that it was a promise that would be kept. The promise gave Americans hope and the people of the Philippines hung to every word of that promise. Everyone knew, they just knew that he would return.

On 29 October 1944 the promise was fulfilled when General MacArthur, "The American Caesar," disembarked on Filipino soil and said "People of the Philippines, I have returned." It was a perfectly orchestrated and dramatic triumphal return! It became a media event. MacArthur's return was captured in pictures and films by newspapers and newsreels. Although total victory was not yet won, "I have returned" became symbolic of ultimate victory. Such is the power of a promise kept!

A promise made and a promise kept are two sides of the same coin. One assumes the other. A promise made and a promise kept has transformational power. While a promise made gives hope to the hearer, its fulfillment empowers the recipient of the promise to rise to new levels of personal fulfillment. Life takes on new and exciting possibilities. Victory can become complete. As one anticipates the fulfillment of a promise, plans are made as new possibilities unfold.

In contrast, unfulfilled promises demoralize and rob us of life's special experiences. When a promise is not kept, dreams are shattered. When vows are broken relationships are deeply scarred and sometimes destroyed. Our children are especially vulnerable to the promises and commitments we make but never fulfill.

Why do we need to be reminded of the importance of keeping our promises? Well, we don't have to go very far to see the results of a promise not kept. Court dockets are overloaded with lawsuits. Rates of divorce continue to hover at about fifty percent. Our adolescent population is plagued with alcohol and drug abuse. Domestic violence shatters lives and hearts in many households and every now and then, the blight of racial discord disrupts our land. The list can go on.

But please… allow me to remind you that I am an eternal optimist, otherwise I would not be in my profession. I truly believe that a person can decide to be a promise keeper. I also believe that there are enough promise keepers in the land to set an example and make a difference. Undoubtedly, there is plenty of room for improvement.

In his engaging book, The Power of a Promise Kept, (focus on the family, 1995), Gregg Lewis points out that being a person of ethical integrity is one of the outstanding characteristics of a Promise Keeper. While his book is addressed to men, ethical integrity must be equally practiced by both genders if we are to be promise keepers.

> ·✛· *Those who have served well gain an excellent standing and great assurance in their faith in Christ Jesus.*
>
> *(1 Timothy 3:13)*

## EXCELLENCE PERSONIFIED

THE INFORMATION COMES from one of many divorce courts in the country. It is the story of a psychoanalyst who wanted to create the perfect wife. He wanted to mold her mind and guide every action to make her achieve perfection. During the divorce proceedings the doctor testified that the "perfect" wife refused to wash the dishes. She wouldn't sweep the house and he often had to baby sit. The wife countercharged that he was not so perfect a husband either. She complained that while he earned $150,000 per year, he only gave her $10.00 per day for personal spending. That's what happened to the marriage of the psychoanalyst and the perfect wife that he desired to create.... And oh by the way, the doctor had made a critical error at the inception of his great experiment. He admitted that he had failed to start by psychoanalyzing himself.

Indeed! The doctor realized that any effort in analyzing others must always begin with a close analysis of the self. However, the million-dollar question is, what is our standard of measurement? To what do we compare ourselves in making sure that we are being objective and accurate?

As you may have gathered from this article's title, the topic is "excellence." This is not an easy topic for me to write about because excellence is closely related to perfection and I'm not a subject matter expert on "perfection." As my wife would quickly affirm, I'm not perfect. Should anyone ever wonder if I'm perfect, please speak with her some time. She will be glad to clarify the matter for you.

I chose this topic of "excellence" because I'm convinced that in each of us there exists an innate desire for excellence. Whether we like it or not or believe in it or not, it's there! Optimists as well as pessimists share in this inner drive to excel. While the optimist will invent the airplane the pessimist will invent the "perfect" parachute. While for many excellence is a dormant quality, we all possess the inner conditions to strive for excellence and reach out for that which is true, noble, right, lovely, admirable and…excellent. Excellence implies that there is an absolute standard that lies beyond us.

Where does this desire come from? I believe it comes from our design as human beings, uniquely created. This desire is intuitive in us. I believe that it is a godly attribute implanted in each of us and we can spend an entire lifetime striving for and developing excellence.

How can we develop excellence? Think, speak and act in ways that are consistent with a person of integrity. A good place to start is The Golden Rule, "treat others as you would like them to treat you." Another natural point of reference is the time-tested core values of Honor, Courage and Commitment (US Navy core values).

Think honorably. Speak with the courage of your convictions and act in such a way as to express your commitment to the right values.

What is its purpose? Its purpose is none other than to bring out the very best that we have to offer the people around us, be it at home with family or in our chosen profession. Its purpose is to self actualize our potential and glorify God through self-development and service. Achieving this purpose requires a fresh and spontaneous spirit in us. Abraham Maslow, famous behavioral psychologist, expressed it in this fashion: "The creativeness of self-actualizers is like that of unspoiled children."

Where does it lead us? The road towards excellence is sprinkled with diamonds. The pay-off comes as we acknowledge our ability to choose freely and thereby bring about positive changes in our lives. So...*Whatever is true, noble, right, pure, lovely...admirable – if anything is excellent and praiseworthy – think about such things.* (Ephesians 4:8)

⊹ *Come to me, all you who are weary and burdened,*
  *and I will give you rest.*
                                      *(Matthew 11:28)*

## GOING THE SECOND MILE

SOME TIME BACK I remember reading about volunteerism in America. I remember reading about people that have gone the extra mile to help others. These were people that were just trying to make the world a kinder and gentler place. For instance, there was a man in New York City who gathered, repaired, and handed out used winter gloves to homeless people in the city. There was

156

another in Virginia who collected farmers' discarded potatoes and delivered them to food kitchens for the poor.

Some were recognized for their tireless and selfless efforts. Most were not. There was no financial pay-off. There were no fancy banquets in their honor attended by politicians and other dignitaries. These people simply stuck their necks out and went the second mile. They went beyond the boundaries of what was expected from them. Many still do. They may appear radical and some may seem a little eccentric in their focused zeal towards volunteerism. For them going the second mile is second nature.

When we examine volunteerism and the potential for liberating the human spirit we will discover that the volunteer is as much blessed as the recipient of his/her service. Indeed, the old adage becomes self evident in volunteerism: "it is more blessed to give than to receive."

Or how about this old expression of wisdom: "If someone forces you to go one mile, go with him two miles." Here is where we need to pay attention. In this saying we find the overriding ethic for helping those in need. I'll even go further, to say that going the second mile is the ultimate measurement of "love" in action.

The historical origin of "going the second mile" is interesting. This aphorism originated during the Roman occupation of Palestine in the first century AD. At the time, the common citizenry of Palestine could be forced into the service of the Romans. They could be compelled to supply food, lodging and even carry a soldier's gear while on a march. It could be a humiliating experience. The command to carry a soldier's pack for one Roman mile (1,000 paces) was legally binding. The adage says: go the one-mile (compulsory) but then volunteer to go a second mile. Why? The second mile was an opportunity to make a friend and disarm your opponent. It's good, practical advice.

Going the extra mile takes us beyond the average and as we volunteer to help others it propels us to a new and higher level of living. When we volunteer in community programs it can overcome our drudgery. We'll become self-starters and we will see our lives change as well as the life of others.

When we become volunteers in our communities, we'll rise above our limitations. When going the second mile becomes second nature in us it will contribute to our personal growth and the progress of others.

It is interesting, but volunteerism tends to overthrow wrongs that may have been done to us. It will focus on, and bring out what is true, and right in us (individually). It will help us to put the past behind. We'll rise above any past resentment because we're focusing on the importance of doing good to benefit others. Volunteerism has the power of vindication.

Think about it. Our lives are truly blessed in so many ways. We possess good health, a steady income, a standard of living and time to enjoy it. Be a volunteer and go the second mile!

·✝· *Trust in the LORD and do good; dwell in the land and enjoy safe pasture. Delight yourself in the LORD and he will give you the desires of your heart. Commit your way to the LORD; trust in him and he will do this: He will make your righteousness shine like the dawn, the justice of your cause like the noonday sun.*

*(Psalm 37:3-6)*

## THE SATISFIED LIFE

YEARS AGO THE popular vocalist Hank Williams sang a song enti-tled "I can't get no satisfaction." Years later the Rolling Stones picked up on it as well. Maybe the grammar "ain't no good." Perhaps you may not like the recording artists for any number of reasons. Nev-ertheless, there is no mistake about the message of their song. For many people today, living the satisfied life can be an elusive goal.

After all, we all want the satisfied, fulfilled life, don't we? Having the right career, getting the best education and experiencing a stable family and home-life are all part of the American dream. There is nothing wrong with desiring these things. Even after achiev-ing certain goals there may still be that certain sense of dissatis-faction, for one discovers that there is no pot of gold at the end of the rainbow. There is always another mountain to climb and there always exists the possibility of failure. This can precipitate a crisis moment in life in which we will ask ourselves: "why don't I have more of a sense of satisfaction?" "I can't get no satisfaction" becomes an uncomfortable reality.

This dilemma can even affect the "faith-full" among us. We may start by questioning the faith which we testify to. The crisis hits as we delude ourselves into thinking that our faith no longer satis-fies. In our self-pity we may even declare that despite our faithful-ness and hard work, it appears that the "bad guys" always seem to get the good stuff.

How in the world do we deal with that? How can we ever embrace the satisfied life? Well, we can address the problem in dif-ferent ways. We can perpetuate the pity party. We can withdraw into a bottomless ocean of remorse or we can even get mad and blame God. One other and much better alternative is to seek out a sincere response to this dilemma of the spirit and realize that the satisfied life can be achieved. The 37th Psalm offers one such response for those of us who "can't get no satisfaction." In its uniquely poetic style, Psalm 37 gives a "shot-gun" approach to discovering the satisfied life. The Psalm's inimitable godly wisdom asks the question: Can I find satisfaction in this life? It then points us to a formula for finding our satisfaction:

1. TRUST IN GOD:

> "Trust in the Lord and do good; dwell in the land and enjoy safe pasture." (Verse 3)

> The word "trust" is synonymous with the word "faith." In fact, to trust is to put our faith into action. As we trust in the things of God our focus (where we fix our mind and heart) will determine our general outlook. As for the evil we may observe around us, we can rest assured that those who harbor evil and injustice in their hearts can anticipate an empty and dismal end.

2. DELIGHT IN THE LORD:

> "Delight yourself in the Lord and he will give you the desires of your heart." (Verse 4)

> This assures us that as a people of faith we can have as much of God as we wish! However, there is a condition attached. That is, we can have as much of God as we wish "if" we delight in the things of God. How can we take delight in God? Well, for starters we can decide to affirm that in spite our circumstance

160

*God still has a purpose for our lives. The ultimate adventure is to pursue and discover that purpose throughout our lives' journey. Each moment of personal discovery becomes a delight-filled experience of God's good grace.*

*In addition, as we TRUST IN GOD, DELIGHT IN GOD and...*

3. COMMIT OURSELVES TO GOD... The Almighty will fulfill the cause/mission of our lives for which we were intended. ("God will make your righteousness shine like the dawn..." verse 6).

   *To be sure, we have not yet lived long enough to see what God will do with us and through us before He is done. If we desire God, if we really desire God, if we really, really delight in God, then we will not desire anything that will put us in opposition to God.*

   ⊹ *Even when I am old and gray, do not forsake me, O God, until I declare your power to the next generation, your might to all who are to come.*

   *(Psalm 71:18)*

## AN ODE FOR THE AGED

FOR A MINUTE I was tempted to title this article, "The Five B's of Old Age: Baldness, Bursitis, Bifocals, Bulges, and Bunions." Occasionally we like to poke fun at the aging process because it may just be a way of poking fun at ourselves. To be sure, regardless of our age, we are all aging.

Life presents us with numerous possibilities and a handful of inevitabilities and aging is one of them. As I prepare to celebrate my birthday in the coming days, I've become introspective about aging. The other day I started to analyze my face in a double width mirror. I noticed the subtle inception of wrinkles around my eyes whenever I smile. There was even the hardly-noticeable presence of fatty growth around my eyes. I immediately remembered a little sign in a gift shop: "When you get too old for pimples you go right into wrinkles." There is no turning back the clock. All the "magic crèmes," lotions or potions cannot turn back the aging process.

However, I am prepared to celebrate the blessings and gifts of encouragement that the elderly have brought to my life. I am prepared to celebrate the nobility, the spiritual depths and integrity that senior adults contribute to our communities. Senior adults have been the gatekeepers of our most cherished values and defenders of our freedoms in our nations past conflicts. To them we owe the preservation of our national heritage. We can learn much from those societies that hold their elderly population in esteemed and honored status.

Yes, I am even prepared to emulate the faithfulness of those senior adults that have modeled spiritual and moral stamina for me. I've learned much from them of what it means to trust in God during good and bad times. The heritage they passed to me has been invaluable. I have learned that whatever life holds, God would always be there for me. Senior adults have been living examples of spiritual realities.

We are now happily young and healthy. In the not too distant future we shall be ranked among the elderly in our society. Thirty to fifty years from now some young writer will be recording observations about us. What will be written? Will we be found faithful? Will our generation be celebrated as defenders of morality, spiritual and ethical integrity? Well that is up to each of us individually as we pass on a positive heritage. Remember that we have a responsibility to the next generation.

A good friend, who is a senior adult, recently shared the following humorous anecdote with me:

"Seniors Are Worth a Fortune:

Remember, old folks are worth a fortune, silver in their hair, gold in their teeth, stones in their kidneys, lead in their feet and gas in their stomachs. I have become a little older since I saw you last and a few changes have come into my life since then. Frankly, I have become quite a frivolous old gal. I'm seeing five gentlemen every day. As soon as I wake up, Will Power helps me out of bed. Then I go to see John. Then Charlie Horse comes along. When he is here, he takes all my time and attention. When he leaves, Arthur Ritis shows up and stays the rest of the day. He doesn't like to stay in one place very long, so he takes me from joint to joint. After such a busy day, I'm really tired and glad to go back to bed with Ben Gay. What a life! P.S. The preacher came to call the other day. He said at my age I should be thinking about the hereafter. I told him I do all the time. No matter where I am, in the parlor, upstairs, in the kitchen, or down in the basement, I ask myself, 'now what am I here after?'" (Author-Anonymous)

Whenever you have the opportunity, have some coffee with a senior adult or volunteer at a senior adult center. Listen to their stories and learn from their experiences.

# SECTION VIII
## COMMUNICATION

 *For by your words you will be acquitted, and by your words you will be condemned."*
*(Matthew 12:37)*

### More Powerful than the Sword

I DON'T KNOW if you have ever had the experience of stumbling over words or making a fool out of yourself in a public speech. How about wondering what to say next when engaged in conversation with a friend or an acquaintance? Sometimes we may feel that our words are not having any effect on those people we're trying to reach.

What if we were to suddenly lose our ability to speak? We would not be able to articulate our feelings, our desires, our joys or even our anger. We would lose the ability to correct false impressions or share our ideas. We would lose the power to encourage, inspire or even reprimand when necessary. We would be forced into a shell of our own inner world and it would be a pretty lonely place.

Even with the ability to speak we run into those awkward moments as we become frustrated with the ineffectiveness of our own words. While many of life's challenges and frustrations may appear to have nothing to do with words, I suggest that words play a very important role, for the use of our words will paint a picture of the emotional, moral and spiritual condition of our soul. That condition will determine how we deal with the issues of life.

The wisdom of the ages has much to say about the use of words. The proverbs of antiquity address the importance that words carry. For example, here is a tested and true statement that echoes from the past:

"For by your words you will be acquitted, and by your words you will be condemned." (Gospel of Matthew 12:37)

This got my attention. It caught my eye and made me reflect about the use of my words. From this simple verity, we can derive a universe of principles that can convict us of our responsibility. Here are some tested principles:

1.  WORDS CAN BLESS: Think of those people who have made a difference in your life.

    *Those people have used words to encourage, motivate and affirm you. Those people have been and may continue to be the "cheerleaders" in your life. Whenever you have been ready to quit, that one special person has had a knack for coming alongside you and utter those special words that have kept you going. Notice that when that happens, their intent is to transform us and bless us with words. That's powerful! We likewise can bless others through the use of our words.*

2. WORDS CAN DESTROY: "Sticks and stones may break my bones but words can never hurt me." It's a nice rhyme but words can hurt and words can destroy reputations. Sticks and stones can't. Marriages can be destroyed and friendships can be crippled when careless words have been used.

3. WORDS WILL DEFINE US: Words will give away who we are.

   *Think about conversations you've had and the image that has been projected by the words we use. Many times words can determine who you become because your words have the power to change your life.*

Rabbi Stephen Samuel Wise was invited to address an anti-Nazi group in Brooklyn. He received several death threats from hate groups. Rabbi Wise mounted the podium on the day of the meeting and said: "I have been warned to stay away from this meeting under pain of being killed. If anyone is going to shoot me, let him do it now. I hate to be interrupted." The good rabbi knew the power of words! He had something to say and his enemies recognized the power behind his words.

Do words have power? YES! Words can change your world and the world of people around you!

⊹ *Finally, brothers, whatever is true, whatever is noble, whatever is right, whatever is pure, whatever is lovely, whatever is admirable—if anything is excellent or praiseworthy—think about such things.*

*(Philippians 4:8)*

## WHATEVER IS TRUE, NOBLE, ADMIRABLE....

I THINK YOU will agree that pollution has become a frustrating problem throughout the planet. It is ironic that while we all suffer from it, we have all contributed to it and continue to do so. Yes, pollution takes many forms but there is one particular type of pollution that is often overlooked. In fact, there are very few laws on the books to try to control it. By the way, we also manage to contribute to it periodically. It is called "Verbal Pollution."

For some of us, verbal pollution has been affecting us since childhood. It starts by invading our thinking and ultimately expresses itself through communication that can become profane and destructive. It is sometimes expressed through idiomatic or slang expressions, which may sound funny /cute but are nonetheless profane.

How many of us would be ashamed to admit the number of times that we've allowed profane thoughts to enter our minds, invade our speech and distort the innate value of a person through some disparaging remark? We need to be reminded often that "stinking thinking" which produces verbal pollution can be replaced by a renewing of our minds for the sake of healthier lives and rewarding relationships.

The process must begin with a renewal of the mind. Why? Because our thinking will affect our communication and communication was given to us by the Creator to make us distinctly human. Therefore, let us renew and revamp the power of our thinking followed by the expression of our words. For if we think in those things which are true, noble, right, lovely, admirable and excellent, the words that follow will be a window to our soul. In effect, we will have the power to bless others knowing that words have the power to bless or condemn.

Indeed, words are a wonderful gift. We can express joy, sadness and everything else in-between. What if we were to suddenly lose the power to speak? We would not be able to encourage and inspire others. We would be forced into a shell, an inner world where our thinking would be trapped.

Our innate ability to communicate is designed to "build-up" and not destroy. Think of those people who have made a difference in our formation. They have encouraged, motivated and inspired us to be the best we can be. Even today there are those who continue to be cheerleaders in our lives. Their thinking, their words and actions affirm, edify and bless us. But, I must return to the foundation of it all because it all begins with proper thinking.

The other side of the coin is that words can and will destroy others. Words can hurt and destroy reputations. As we reflect on those painful experiences in our lives we will find that much hurt has been inflicted by people we have trusted who have used words as a deadly weapon. Their words may have sought to devalue us or undermine our good intentions. The best of relationships may have been destroyed by words. Perhaps at some point we have used words to undermine others and have found ourselves minus a few friends. Again, it all starts with the kind of thinking that can either bless or destroy.

The process must start with me, the individual. It must begin in the very core of my being as I decide, daily, to replace the destructive forces of negative thinking with the positive power of thoughts which are true, noble, right, admirable and excellent.

Admittedly, this is not easy to accomplish but it is worth every ounce of our efforts. Robert Schuller identified the releasing power of this possibility when he stated, "We can discover the power of words to change our lives." Indeed, we can change a world through it.

Do you believe that? I do!

·✦· *Like a city whose walls are broken down is a man
who lacks self-control.*

*(Proverbs 25:28)*

## Yellow Light-Red Light- Green Light

IN HIS BOOK Healing Heart, author Norman Cousins relates a conflict he encountered some years ago with a telephone operator. He had lost a quarter while attempting a call at a pay phone. A recording came on and asked him for another quarter. He inserted another quarter and a live operator picked up the line. Mr. Cousins told her what had happened and the operator responded that the phone company would be glad to send him the quarter if he would give her his name and address. Well, it seemed ridiculous that the phone company would spend the postage plus labor just to refund him a quarter and he told her so. Therefore, he pressed the coin return lever and at that point, all the guts of the machine opened up. Quarters, nickels and dimes came tumbling out. "Operator," he said, "are you still there?" "Yes" she answered. "Operator, something unbelievable has just happened. All I did was press the coin return lever and the phone is giving me all its money. There must be more than five dollars in coins here and the flow hasn't stopped." "Sir, will you please put the money back in the box?" She said. "Operator, if you will give me your name and address, I'll be glad to mail it to you." .... Touché!

Hey, have you been there? Have you ever found yourself in the middle of frustrating conversations? This exchange with the operator reminds us of how frustrating it can be to communicate with some people. When the signal lights of good communication get short-circuited, we find ourselves going from the yellow warning light that something is wrong to the red light of anger. Once we are in the red light zone things tend to escalate. We will be drawn deeper into the pit of emotions and it may become increasingly more difficult to defuse the situation. Let's take a few moments to take inventory of our temper gauge. Let's do some preventive maintenance on our equipment (signal lights of temper). Let's then make adjustments and improvements on our communication skills and emotional temperament. In doing so we'll preserve our friendships and maybe make some new ones along the way. Let's take another look at the signal lights:

THE YELLOW LIGHT OF SELF PROTECTION.
*In conventional traffic the yellow is the warning light advising us to start coming to a halt. It's designed for self protection. If we decide to attempt driving through it, we may find ourselves going through the red light and possibly have an accident. Emotionally speaking, the yellow light is likewise a warning. It can assist us in our relationships by warning us that something may be wrong and needs to be resolved. It is a warning that we need to take pause before things begin to escalate. It is an opportunity to talk things out, to clear the air of any misunderstandings and even express an apology if necessary. When*

we're at the yellow light, we proceed with care. If we ignore the yellow light and go through it, we'll find ourselves in…

THE RED LIGHT OF ANGER. *This can be dangerous. When we're there, we can say and do things to others that become extremely difficult, if not impossible to take back. It puts us on an emotional "slippery slope." One angry remark leads to another. We can make dreadful mistakes by fooling ourselves into thinking that anger is an instrument of strength when in fact it can be an indication of a profound weakness and fear. The proverbs of antiquity express it well: "Like a city whose walls are broken down is a man who lacks self control" (Holy Bible, Proverbs 25:28). But there is recovery in…*

THE GREEN LIGHT OF GOD'S WISDOM. *This "wisdom" is not technical knowledge and is not acquired in a university. It is the ability to do what is right in the face of moral dilemmas. It is the ability to interpret circumstances in light of God's eternal values. How do you get it? It happens as one submits to God and resists evil. As one draws near to God, God will draw nearer. The by-product is integrity, personal peace and lack of fear. Now that, my friends, is worth having!*

·✠· *My dear brothers, take note of this: Everyone should be quick to listen, slow to speak and slow to become angry.…*

*(James 1:19)*

## QUICK TO LISTEN, SLOW TO SPEAK

A MAN WENT to his neighborhood barber for a haircut. The barber was one of those "little people" always cutting others down to size. He was the type of person with always something negative to say. He just loved to discourage. The customer sat down for his cut and proceeded to tell the barber that he was taking a trip to Rome. The barber's response was typically negative: "Well, I hear that Rome is over-rated. The hotels are overpriced. The streets are a nightmare to drive in and Italians are rude to Americans. You'll hate the trip. You're throwing your money away!" The customer protested: "But I've been saving my money for years. Besides, there's a good chance that I'll be able to get an audience with the Pope." "I wouldn't count on it if I were you," said the barber. "The Pope only gives audiences to really important people."

A few weeks later the man returned to the barbershop. "Well how was the trip?" asked the barber, sarcastically. "Rome was beautiful. The hotels were outstanding and the Italians were super friendly. Hey, I even got to see the Pope!" The barber couldn't believe it. "You got to see the Pope? What happened?" "That's right, I even bent down and kissed his ring," said the customer. "Wow! Did the Pope say anything?" asked the barber. "Yes, he did. He looked down at my head while I was kneeling and said 'what a lousy haircut!'"

You ever get into those kinds of unending exchanges with seemingly difficult people? It's called "one-upmanship." It is the kind of antagonism that can escalate into aggression that doesn't help in winning friends and influencing people. These exchanges have a tendency to escalate until we allow the subtle exchanges to turn into ugly, abrasive confrontations.

Things are said, feelings are trampled and then after this catharsis of emotions and anger take place, we find ourselves at a loss and maybe even feel defeated. These kinds of experiences invade the tranquility of our lives. It can lead us to ask important questions such as, how can I avoid conflict? If in a tense relationship, how can I apply principles to keep me walking the high road? How can I manage conflict to preserve friendships and rise above the situation? After all, differences of opinion and interpersonal conflicts are inevitable. Well, here are some principles that have helped me in managing conflict. When applied, these principles can diminish conflict and help to keep a few friends:

BE QUICK TO LISTEN. Communication theorists emphasize the use of the receivers (ears). Common sense points out the importance of listening. The problem arises when we allow the mouth to work twice as much as the ears. As we listen, we need to listen with the "inner" ear of the heart and try to identify what the speaker is truly addressing. We then assume responsibility for those things that we can fix and whenever necessary have the integrity to apologize when we are at fault.

BE SLOW TO SPEAK. In his classic work "How to Win Friends and Influence People," Dale Carnegie wrote, "Criticism is futile because it puts a person on the defensive and usually makes him strive to justify himself. Criticism is dangerous because it wounds a person's precious pride, hurts his sense of importance and arouses resentment…. Any fool can criticize, condemn and complain – and most fools do. But it takes character and self control to be understanding and forgiving." Now, that's good advise!

BE SLOW TO BECOME ANGRY. Anger has the power to divide and destroy friendships. However, is anger normal? Yes! Anger is an indicator pointing out that something is wrong and needs fixing. Allowed to run its course anger is an energy force that will deplete our pool of positive energy. We must harness anger and convert it into a positive force. This process begins with forgiveness and restoration. This assumes the other party's willingness to return in kind. When the other party insists in their belligerence, we do have the inherent right to disengage ourselves and seek protection. Admittedly, these things are not easy to do. Nevertheless, when applied consistently there is great potential for personal freedom and an inner peace that transcends all understanding. PEACE!

# SECTION IX
## LOVE & MARRIAGE &....

 *Let him kiss me with the kisses of his mouth—for your love is more delightful than wine.*
*(Song of Solomon 1:2)*

## WHAT'S LOVE GOT TO DO WITH IT?
## (ON VALENTINE'S DAY)

THE LATE JOHN Lennon of the legendary Beetles expressed it this way:

· Love is real · Love is wanting · Love is free
real is love to be love … free is love …
· Love is feeling · Love is knowing
feeling love we can be

The name of the song was "LOVE." It sold millions. But the words leave you in an ocean of ambiguity and ultimately beg the question: "What is love?"

In the mid 1970's the nation was spell-bound and teary-eyed by the classic movie "Love Story." Its most memorable line was "Love means never having to say you're sorry" (sure...). And of course, we have Tina Turner's famous rendering of the cynical side of human emotions and relations in her hit song "What's Love Got to do with it?" Although fatalistic in tone, Tina's interpretation of the song brings us the closest to dealing with the question. That question needs to be addressed, most especially on this day.

Valentine's Day begs the question: "What is love, anyway?" Is it purely an emotion resulting from an experience? Is it based upon seeking pleasure and avoiding pain? After the "warm and fuzzies" wear off, can love be found?

Well, as an ordained Christian minister I would be negligent in addressing this question without referring to one of the greatest passages ever written on the topic. Indeed, it is one of the most sublime expressions on this subject to be found in the Bible. So, please indulge me if but for a few moments. It's the Apostle Paul's greatest dissertation on the subject of love:

*Love is patient, love is kind, it does not envy, it does not boast, it is not proud. It is not rude, it is not self-seeking, it is not easily angered, it keeps no record of wrongs. Love does not delight in evil, but rejoices with the truth. It always protects, always trusts, always hopes, always perseveres. Love never fails... these three remain: faith, hope, and love. But the greatest of these is love. (I Corinthians13: 4-8a, NIV)*

This passage is so appropriate because it addresses all humanity regardless of your religious affiliation. Hey, you can even be an atheist and subscribe to its pronouncements! This is truly a universal message and points us to the greatest "idea" ever: LOVE. Do you want to know what love is? Read, study and apply this passage. It doesn't take long to figure out that above all love is made up of two basic realities:

1.  Love is a decision
2.  Love is a commitment.

When the decision and commitment to love is made daily, then love never fails. Love becomes a bonding agent that time, space and circumstances cannot change. Love holds the house together. It is the nails and paint used on a house. The nails hold the house together. The paint beautify and preserve the material.

Love always protects as we look after each other. We trust together and hope together through a common vision. We persevere together as the stronger holds up the weaker, as we comfort each other and strengthen each other. We are patient, as we understand that change is part of life and we work with each other through the changes. We forgive and let go. We also must be ready to seek forgiveness whenever necessary. What a wonderful revelation we have here. After all, it teaches me that learning to love is not a destination but it is a commitment and a daily decision of the will.

What does love have to do with it? Everything!

⁜ *Let love and faithfulness never leave you; bind them around your neck, write them on the tablet of your heart.*

*(Proverbs 3:3)*

## "AIN'T" LOVE GRAND?

THEY WERE YOUNG (he was 19, she was 18), handsome and very much in love. One day while looking through the Sunday newspaper, they spotted a full-page ad. It announced the annual kissing contest to take place at the senior high school in town. The object of the contest was to determine which couple could remain locked in a kiss the longest.

They were so madly in love that they felt absolutely certain to be the next champions. After all, they had lots of practice. The young couple filled out the entry form. On the day of the contest they, along with the other couples, arrived and got "in position."

"On your mark, get set…. 'Smack.'" Fifteen minutes elapsed … 45 minutes … 90 minutes…. 105 minutes and 48 seconds. Our young couple was the only contestants left standing. All others had dropped out. They were the new champions and had even broken the record! They would have kept going but… wouldn't you believe it? They keeled over and dropped to the ground, unconscious.

An ear, nose and throat specialist rushed over to examine them. The doctor quickly determined that they had fainted due to lack of oxygen! "Ain't" love grand?

The things that love makes us do can get us into some rather silly, comical and sometimes humiliating predicaments. Yet, we submit ourselves to the task of searching for love. Without love in our lives there is a significant void. There is in each of us a desire to love and to be loved. When we fail to love properly, we will either turn against ourselves or turn against others.

A great paradox exists in our culture. In all of history, humanity has never been surrounded by so much recreational and social activities. In spite of this, many people suffer from loneliness. In one year the average American meets as many people as the average person did in a lifetime 200 years ago. However, I suspect that people are far lonelier in modern times. This should not surprise us. After all, we live in a culture that teaches and encourages total independence and self-assurance. Some personal relationships can tend to be banal and superficial. The result is a culture that almost has a neurotic desire to be loved but yet rejects intimacy.

Well, let's face it. To truly love and engage in meaningful relationships can be intimidating. In loving unconditionally we have to

come to terms with our ego and pride. In our effort to love unconditionally we will face moments of failure because of our built-in
imperfections. In those moments of failure we can experience God's
love through the unconditional love and forgiveness of others.

There is a great promise for those who love unconditionally. The
promise is that love casts out all fear.... All fear! What a remarkable promise. As love matures on a day-to-day basis, the result is
that fear is cast out because love replaces it. It is offered unconditionally, with no strings attached.

History has passed down to us a wonderful story about a great
Christian of the 13th century: Francis of Assisi. Francis was ter-
rified of leprosy. Just thinking of it horrified him. One day while
walking alone along a path in the woods, he saw a leper walking
towards him. His reaction was instinctive. He felt nothing but
rejection and disgust. But, at the same time he felt ashamed of his
feelings. Francis walked towards the man, threw his arms around
his neck and kissed his cheek. A moment later he looked back and
there was no one there, only an empty road. All the days of his
life Francis was convinced that, through that experience, God had
tested his capacity to love unconditionally.

There is no greater standard in evaluating our lives except by the
standard of loving as God loves (unconditionally). Those who can
truly love have energy to live. To love means to forgive, to restore,
to reconcile, to obey (love your neighbor as yourself). "Ain't" love
grand?

⁙ *May your father and mother be glad; may she who
gave you birth rejoice!*

*(Proverbs 23:25)*

## THE MOTHER OF ALL ARTICLES

OKAY, NOW THAT I have your attention, allow me to proceed. The first Persian Gulf War still resonates in our collective memory. As our armed forces mobilized a momentum started to build up which would reach a climax. You may also remember that people tended to be more spiritual. The old maxim, "there are no atheists in foxholes" rang truer in those days. As the moment of ultimate confrontation approached, the leader of Iraq, Saddam Hussein, described the anticipated encounter as "The Mother of all Battles."

When I first heard the expression, I couldn't help laughing. It sounded funny. But let's look at the meaning of this superlative expression. In this context it is pretty obvious that the use of the word "mother" meant something along the lines of "overwhelming," "immense," "spectacular," "awesome."

Now, the word "mother" is worthy of those kinds of thoughts. Motherhood truly defies comparison. I should think that on Mothers Day, every chaplain across the land should desire to write "The Mother of All Articles." I don't know if you've noticed but mothers and chaplains have a great deal in common. I know that I don't look like your mother but both chaplains and mothers commit their lives to trying to get people to do what they don't want to do in order that they might become what they've always wanted to become. Mothers are change agents and chaplains try to be. Mothers and chaplains appreciate being affirmed and recognized but think we would prefer that people follow what we preach rather than honoring what we do. Mothers and chaplains seek to nurture growth and personal development in those entrusted to us. The approaches are sometimes gentle, other times challenging and from time to time disturbing. Mothers and chaplains may get ignored and sometimes insulted but deep down inside remains a genuine concern for the people around us. At times a chaplain, like a mother, is not the best friend you have. Sometimes he/she is the only friend you have.

However, nothing truly and totally parallels the inimitable reality of motherhood. I therefore celebrate all Mothers Days with a thankful heart for the gift of motherhood and the gifts that these special women have brought to our lives. Mark Twain once said, "my mother had a great deal of trouble with me. But I think she enjoyed it!" What he meant was that she enjoyed the forgiving and restoring. I can relate to this. From my mother I received the gift of forgiveness. Indeed, I came to understand God's capacity to forgive through my mother's enormous capacity to forgive me. Experiencing her forgiveness taught me to live and grow with a sense of confidence and certainty that everything was all right. I came to understand the value of perseverance through a mother who would not give up on her God-given responsibilities. She taught me a few things about patience and spiritual endurance.

In William Gibson's classic work *Mass for the Dead* he writes about the events surrounding his mother's demise. After her death, he yearned for the faith that upheld her wonderful life. It was a faith that held-up during a difficult death. He took up her gold-rimmed glasses, her faded, well used Bible and sat in her favorite chair. He wanted to experience what had so deeply centered and empowered her. Her impact profoundly influenced his life. That, my friends, is powerful mentoring! Let's celebrate the gift of motherhood!

✙ *Husbands, love your wives, just as Christ loved the church and gave himself up for her.*
*(Ephesians 5:25)*

## PUCKER-UP, DAD

THERE WAS ONCE a husband who was somewhat confused about the important subject of loving his wife to provide a stable home for his children. His wife suffered from depression and was always upset and unhappy. The concerned husband took her to a psychiatrist. After listening attentively to the couple, he prescribed the proper treatment with the following demonstration. He went over to the man's wife, gathered her up in his arms, and gave her a big kiss. The woman's reaction was spontaneous as she looked at the doctor with a glowing face and a broad smile. The doctor turned to the husband and said, "You see! All she needs is a little love." Expressionless, the husband said, "Okay, Doc. I can bring her in on Tuesdays and Thursdays."

Yes, I know.... Fathers Day is over. Then, why am I writing about this? The point is very simple. We have a very, very short memory. I believe that Fathers Day would even be a grander celebration if we kept in mind some compelling realities regarding the responsibilities of fatherhood throughout the entire year. Fathers Day presents us with the opportunity to analyze our effectiveness as fathers. I believe that the measure of a good Fathers Day is determined not by how many gifts we fathers received from our kids but by how much we have given of ourselves throughout the year. We need to understand that one of the best gifts that we can give our children is a healthy marriage. When fathers love their wives, their children derive great benefits. Children will feel safe and secure. They will learn how to love and how to live.

Do you need another motivator? How about this one: A West German magazine released the fascinating results of a study conducted by a life insurance company a few years ago. The study found that husbands who kiss their wives every morning live an average of five years longer, are involved in fewer car accidents, are ill 50% less, and earn 20 to 30% more money. So husbands, love your wives. It is good for you and for your children.

For married dads, Fathers Day is not so much a question of how much do fathers love their children. I think it is really more of a question of fathers loving their wives. When we love our wives, everyone in the family is a winner...our wives, our children and ourselves. It is wise, it is healthy and it is Scriptural: "Husbands, love your wives...." *(Ephesians 5:25).*

So, "pucker-up" dad!

However, good Fathers Day advice is not only limited to those of us who are married. I also realize that a number of dads live apart from their children. Perhaps they have remarried and started new families. Indeed, in these modern times many single dads are even raising children on their own. This situation does not have to rob those dads of the happiness of being complete in their role as a father. Yes, it will challenge them to be more creative but it can be done successfully if they make the TIME and capture those special opportunities to savor the presence and love that their children long to express. The initiative lies with them and their ability to plan accompanied by the desire to give of themselves. Whether single or married, fatherhood will demand from us our creativity and sacrifice from time to time. It is worth every moment of our efforts.

Life will present us dads with many opportunities to give of ourselves and leave our children a most important legacy: our love and support.

> ⊹ *For no one can lay any foundation other than the one already laid, which is Jesus Christ.*
> *(1 Corinthians 3:11)*

## LITTLE HOUSE ON THE ROCK

PRIME TIME TELEVISION programs that feature the family have been very popular over the years. Family themes have consistently ranked among the top 20 in TV programming. It demonstrates that for millions of Americans the topic of "family" is a primetime priority. Some sociologists have gone as far as theorizing that these programs are some of the prime time shapers of family values in America.

A few years ago there was a program on television (prime time) that featured the late Michael Langdon (of Bonanza fame). It continues to be one of the all-time favorites in TV history. It was called "Little House on the Prairie." What made it so popular were the timeless values that the Ingalls family modeled for its audience. They portrayed values that we all seek to possess and practice in our own families. Love, support, consideration, patience, forgiveness, restoration and hope were among some of the many topics exemplified.

Like any family, the Ingalls had their problems but they managed to work things out. Each episode always moved towards a goal. Each story line went somewhere and its underlying emphasis was always the importance of the family. The Ingalls were always in the process of "building" their family. Their house on the prairie seemed to be built upon a solid foundation of rock. It was a foundation consisting of good morals, concern, love and mutual support. The program had a special way of calling us to mirror these values.

Today the call to action for the family is no less compelling. The 21st century family is challenged to make the choice to build or not to build a house on a foundation of solid rock. You see, anyone can build a house but will it be built on the proper foundation? If you build the structure on a foundation of sand it will not stand.

The sand foundation refers to a wishy-washy, loose commitment to firm convictions in the family.

Please remember that every family builds on a foundation. Every family, and I mean every, will experience storms. Survival in the storms of life will depend on choosing the right foundation. So, in practical terms, how do we build such a house? Well, for starters we build it from reality not fantasy. We must know our strengths and weaknesses as a family. As a fellow builder, let me make some practical suggestions on pouring the foundation.

1. DON'T DEIFY DAD: Don't make a god out of dad. Respect dad but don't worship dad. Worship and reverence is reserved for God alone. The father that puts himself in the position of God in the home is building his family on a foundation of sand. A man building on a solid rock foundation brings home a healthy attitude. Family time is to be respected, protected and used wisely. A solid foundation seeks to edify, compliment and build-up family members. Discipline for the children is used with wisdom, balance and good timing. The goal of discipline is to build up and not tear down.

2. DON'T MODIFY MOM: Don't try to change mom to fit you agenda and expectations. Mom is an original. The Almighty created her and threw away the mold. She has gifts and abilities peculiar to her personality and role in life. Mom can use those special abilities to nurture and show compassion and by doing so model some godly traits that all of us need to experience.

3.  DON'T CODIFY THE KIDS: Let's not try to "clone" our children into something that they are not. Let's celebrate the uniqueness of our children and instead encourage our kids to be the very best they can be with the abilities that they have.

When the family is built on the foundation of solid rock, it becomes a true treasure in our lives. When built on solid foundation the word "family" becomes a holy word. It becomes a sacred reality. Our family is a sacred trust very carefully placed in our hands by God.

> ⊹ *But if serving the LORD seems undesirable to you, then choose for yourselves this day whom you will serve, whether the gods your forefathers served beyond the River, or the gods of the Amorites, in whose land you are living. But as for me and my household, we will serve the LORD."*
>
> *(Joshua 24:15)*

## THE FAMILY: COMMITTED

WAY BACK IN 1990 there was a "T-shirt testimony" making its rounds in the local South Florida market. A number of people wore it proudly with no fear of recrimination or ridicule. You may have seen it. It read: "God Made Notre Dame #1. Miami Made Them #2." Well, it was an arrogant statement and even borderline blasphemous. I'm not too sure if God is in the business of getting involved with national football championships (some of you may disagree).

But, I do know this: there are Divine priorities… and I believe that "family" is a Divine priority. To God the family is precious!

I believe that in the divine order of things the family is sacred. If this is true, and I believe it is, the family is to be protected and cherished. In view of this, the family is also the workshop for applied and practical spirituality. It is the basic unit where we can affirm the goodness of God. No wonder that when things go wrong with the family so much else goes wrong with us individually.

I wonder that if the truth were to be known would we be in agreement with all of the aforesaid? I wonder whether we would, instead, be wearing a T-shirt stating: "God Made The Family #1. I made it #2"?

I'm not a prophet of doom. I believe that chaplains are called to be (among other things) ministers of hope. I believe that chaplains are called to convey a message that will help us to be better. Indeed, that is my goal as I write this article. Nevertheless, sometimes we do have to face some sad facts in the process of arriving at true hope. A very sad fact is that the family is in trouble in our society. The stability of so many families have been threatened and even destroyed through rage, frustration, unhappiness and helplessness. The statistics bear this out. Since the early 1960's violent crimes in families have increased exponentially. The rates of teenage pregnancies, teenage suicides, and divorces reflect the general malaise which undermines the preservation of the family. Anyone of our families can become a casualty.

Whether we have been victims of the attack on the family or not we can all make a new start and rekindle our hope and commitment for the family. We can recapture a vision and a life which is in line with the kinds of values that build-up our families. Here's a primer that I personally review to help me stay the course:

1.  There must be a passion in us that is greater than personal privilege. Is our personal privilege secondary as it relates to the family? How can I serve my family members? How can we render proper respect and honor to those in our families that have always been there for us? All of this translates into expressing appreciation, good communication and identifying those special moments to encourage.

2.  There must be a purpose larger than life. When we have purpose we'll have priorities. When we have purpose we'll put our passion into action. Good purpose will involve us with our family in good ways. When a family shares in a common purpose its priorities and goals will be congruent and productive of "good fruits." A purpose that is "larger than life" strives to leave a legacy of good will and good works to benefit the greater society as well as our posterity. It becomes part of leaving a legacy.

A family that is committed has an orientation that hungers for moral, spiritual and emotional growth. It can become a wonderful journey that never ends.

It would be nice to fashion a T-shirt that states: "God Has Made The Family #1 And I Agree With It."

> ⊹ *Train a child in the way he should go, and when he is old he will not turn from it.*
>
> *(Proverbs 22:6)*

## TRAIN UP A CHILD

IN HIS BOOK *Mistreated*, author Ron Lee Dunn tells about two altar boys. One was born in 1892 in Eastern Europe. The other boy was born 3 years later in a small town in Illinois. Though they lived separate lives in different parts of the world they almost had identical experiences.

Each boy was given the opportunity to assist his parish priest during the service of Communion. Each boy, while handling the Communion cup, accidentally spilled some of the wine on the carpet. There, the similarities end. The priest in the European church, seeing the wine stain on the carpet severely scolded the altar boy shouting: "You clumsy oaf! Leave the altar!" That little boy grew up and became an atheist and a communist. He became the strongman dictator of Yugoslavia from 1943-1980. His name was Josip Broz Tito.

In contrast, the priest at the Illinois church, seeing a similar carpet stain knelt down to the little boy's level, looked at him tenderly in the eyes and said: "It's all-right son. You'll do better next time. Someday, you'll be a fine priest." That little boy grew up to become the much-loved Bishop Fulton Sheen.

Here we have two young boys sharing similar experiences with radically different endings. The author points to the vulnerable and delicate balance that exists in a child's early experiences. Indeed many of us know how difficult it is to overcome early negative experiences.

Imagine this scene with me. A mother sits in a pastor's study. Her eyes are bloodshot red from incessant crying, hands clasped in pain. She commences to talk about her rebellious, run-away teenage daughter. The minister, desiring to comfort, does what she could do best. She reaches for the best council she has available.

She opens the Bible to the book of Proverbs, Chapter 22, verse 6 and reads: "Train up a child in the way he should go and when he is old he will not depart from it." Allow me this simplified version: "It's better to build boys and girls than to repair men and women."

Grant it, many times regardless of our best efforts in teaching our children the right way, they will still make the wrong decisions. Nevertheless, as parents we are still responsible to "train up the child." Our positive or negative influence on our children can have a lasting impact. Our responsibility is tremendous. In assuming our responsibilities we need to avail ourselves of the best wise council of those that have already gone before us. It's a lot less painful to learn from the experience of others. That is why "proverbial" wisdom is so important. The advise maps out a course of action that if followed will assure a degree of success.

If we are to "train up a child" then we are called to teach. In my religious tradition, there exists a cherished ceremony for new babies called "baby dedication." In this ceremony, the parents stand before their congregation (church-family) and commit to raise up the child to know the things of God and to teach the child "the way" to go. Unfortunately, so many parents that follow this tradition have done so out of custom and have not followed the spirit of their commitment.

I believe that the most important teachers that our children will ever have are their parents. In teaching, parents identify with the truth and commit to conveying and living out the truth in their own lives.

Socrates (469-399 BC) expressed it well:

*Could I climb to the highest place in Athens, I would lift my voice and proclaim, 'fellow-citizens, why do ye turn and scrape every stone to gather wealth, and so little care of your children, to whom one day you must relinquish it all?'*

⊹ *In your anger do not sin: Do not let the sun go*
*down while you are still angry, and do not give*
*the devil a foothold.*

*(Ephesians 4:26-27)*

## SAVED BY THE BELL

THERE'S A STORY about a judge in a divorce case who asked the husband: "Sir, will you tell the court what passed between you and your wife during your big argument that caused you to seek this separation?" "Sure. I'll tell you judge. It was a rolling pin, six plates and a frying pan!"

There is something disturbingly true behind this story. Many couples destroy their marriage by engaging in escalating tension-producing behaviors. Failing to keep emotions under control that can become destructive can easily become a bad habit in any marriage. The process of escalation is for the most part progressive. It starts with anger that turns to resentment and then escalates to rage and in some instances manifests itself with verbal, emotional and even physical abuse.

Yes, I know that living with the average family can sometimes be like working in a fireworks factory. At times nothing on earth can exasperate, frustrate or even destroy like family itself. Yet, I truly believe that God has given us our family and its preservation is therefore a sacred responsibility.

In this article I'd like to fight for, not with the family. I would also like to state unconditionally that abuse of any kind is an unacceptable response in the family. The victim of abuse has a legal and moral right to seek protection and hold the perpetrator accountable. I believe that the words "abuse" and "family" are incompatible. However, we find that domestic violence is alarmingly high in our society and that the ability of families to successfully resolve conflict seems to be on the decline.

None of us are exempt from dealing with conflict in our homes. The occasional argument is expected even in the best of all possible worlds. But to allow feelings and emotions to evolve into anger and uncontrollable rage is to be prevented at all costs. The stakes are simply too high.

Have we ever stopped to think that the World Boxing Association has rules for prize fighting but that families rarely do? Yes! Few families fight fair. Yes! No family member ever really wins without somebody losing. Yes! Every couple needs rules and regulations for fighting fairly. So, without further ado, here are some ground rules for fighting fair in the family.

FIRST and foremost, CHECK YOUR WEAPONS AT THE DOOR! In the days of the Wild West men had to check-in their weapons before entering the saloon. This prevented anyone from getting trigger-happy.

Words are our weapons and deadly words are deadly weapons. How we use our words can be a truly devastating thing. Words impulsively and thoughtlessly used will create a wedge in the marriage and may even become impossible to take back. Those words will undermine and seriously hurt our partner. Remember that escalation typically begins with improper words. We can allow those improper words to become profane and abusive. Venomous words will attack the dignity of the spouse. Once we resort to rage and profanity we are announcing our ignorance.

We check our weapons at the door by keeping our language clean and controlled and engage in a process of dialogue. This takes personal discipline and a respect for the spouse's dignity. The goal is to speak the truth in love.

Rest assured that in our midst and within our reach we have tremendous resources to preempt serious escalation of conflict in the family. Never hesitate to access the good advice of qualified marriage and family therapists as well as concerned pastoral counselors.

You can fight the good fight to restore wholeness to your marriage. It will honor your spouse and it will honor God.

⊹ *You turned my wailing into dancing; you removed my sackcloth and clothed me with joy...*
> *(Psalm 30:11)*

## Is there Life after Divorce?

AFTER DECIDING THAT she wanted to divorce her husband, the disillusioned wife went to her best friend for advice. "My husband and I just don't get along!" she said. Her friend thought for a minute and responded, "Why don't you sue for divorce on the grounds of incompatibility?" "Well, I would," said the disillusioned wife, "if only I could catch him at it."

We may snicker at such an anecdote, but divorce is not a laughing matter. Indeed, it is an emotionally painful experience frequently accompanied by feelings of guilt and grief. The wave of grief that may follow divorce is like the grief cycle experienced when losing a loved one to death. To be sure, divorce brings about the termination or death of a relationship. I have yet to meet a person who planned on getting a divorce while saying, "I do" at their wedding ceremony. I have yet to meet anyone who has admitted to having enjoyed getting a divorce even under the worst of conditions in their marital relationship. But, consider the following data: close to fifty percent of first marriages end in divorce. Approximately eighty percent of divorced people remarry within the first two years following their first divorce. Approximately sixty percent of second marriages end in divorce. In the last century the incidence of divorce increased by 700 percent. While the numbers are impressive (and maybe discouraging) they do not even begin to address the financial turmoil that divorce can bring. An ample case can also be made to illustrate the impact of divorce in the lives of many children as well as relatives on both sides of the family. Divorce imposes immense stress on both parties, families, associates and friends. Regardless of the reasons, often, loved ones (including children) are inadvertently forced to choose sides.

As a chaplain I am in the business of marriage fixing versus marriage busting. However, I do realize that as much as I may deplore its existence, divorce is part of the landscape in modern family life. I also realize and affirm that there exist legitimate grounds for seeking a divorce.

Over the years one can find any number of articles in journals and marriage manuals prescribing ways for preventing divorces and fixing marriages. Some of these articles have also listed the reasons that many marriages break up. In this article I want to address the after-effects of a broken marriage. What do you do if you have experienced divorce? How do you recover emotionally and financially from the after-effects? Is there life after divorce? Yes, there is life after divorce and there are ample resources available to help in restoring balance and emotional health. Here are just a few things that can be done:

1. APPEAL TO YOUR SPIRITUAL FOUNDATIONS: Numerous faith-based communities, as well as non-sectarian organizations, provide divorce recovery programs. These sharing and support

groups teach practical principles of application that contain a strong spiritual and moral foundations. Good, church-based programs for divorce recovery will also be non-judgmental and will seek to restore and integrate the individual back into the faith-based community.

2. TAKE STOCK OF YOUR FINANCES: Do not hesitate to consult with a certified financial advisor. Divorce can and will impact one's financial profile. A financial consultant can assist in rearranging finances and in possibly identifying new alternatives.

3. DEVELOP A HEALTHY SOCIAL LIFE: The natural tendency for many divorced people is to start dating immediately after a divorce. I would suggest that cultivating new friendships and reinvigorating some old friendships is a wiser choice. Take pause and allow some time to elapse before jumping back into dating.

4. TAKE STOCK IN YOURSELF: The period following a divorce can present marvelous opportunities for self-discovery. Make the time to consult with a counselor if the need arises. Why not consider taking some of those college courses that were put on the back burner? Get to know yourself better and reaffirm your innate qualities and abilities that make you a unique child of God.

5. TAKE A MOMENT AND LOOK AROUND YOU. As often as you may feel alone, take the time to recognize the wonderful friends and family that God has placed in your life to provide strength and support. As bad and painful as divorce can be, remember

that someone will always have it worse. It is up to you to take the unfortunate occurrence and make it a positive testimony that may hopefully save another relationship or simply serve as a story of inspirational recovery.

YES! There is life after divorce! The choice is yours to make.

# SECTION X
## THE CIVIC VIRTUES

·✦· *Greater love has no one than this, that he lay down*
   *his life for his friends.*

   *(John 15:13)*

### In Remembrance of Them (On 9/11)

IT ALMOST FEELS incredible that we have now had nearly twenty
years for the experience to settle into our collective conscience. I
guess that we could rename the terrorists "the equal opportunity
destroyers." When those four massive airliners crashed into the
Two Towers, the Pentagon and the open field in Pennsylvania, all
the innocent victims shared in one common, terrifying moment.
That experience eliminated all social, religious, economic, racial
and ethnic differences that may have existed. All the souls that perished, perished equally.

Many of those that survived this incomprehensible and cowardly
act saw their world of position, rank, livelihood vanish away. The
visible symbols of their status and careers may have literally evap-
orated. It all truly became a transcendent moment for the survivors

and for us all as we watched, helplessly. As people grieved beyond despair they held in their hands symbols, pictures, personal effects of their loved ones. These symbols helped all of us stay connected with the lives of our patriots.

Yes, I know that sometimes we want the images to go away. Some of us may keep seeing in our minds these terrifying images over and over. But, that singular day has become part of our national fiber and identity as we have embraced the experience and used it to make us a better and stronger people.

The observation has been made that life itself is ultimately made up of symbols. These symbols represent the "stuff" that surround us and define our identity. If there is some truth in this, then the question follows: what are the symbols of your life? If these symbols were destroyed overnight how would you identify the ultimate realities that define your life? Hopefully, we may never again experience the devastation of a 9/11. However, we don't know that. If the crisis comes along and our lives come apart, if devastation takes hold, what will be the transcendent realities about my life? Will I possess "the right stuff"? That is, will others be able to identify the ultimate essence of my life that will remain standing even after the devastation?

Yes, of course these are hard questions. However, I submit to you that these questions strike at the very heart of our identity and purpose. The questions don't get any easier. For instance: How does my lifestyle project the extent to which I've allowed material "things" to shape me? What are you allowing to shape your values? What are the truths that drive the very core of our lives? If I were to suddenly perish, what are the symbols and principles that my friends and loved ones would hold up as representative of my life? Indeed, sobering questions for the thoughtful.

The dear souls that were lost on 9/11 continue to touch our hearts. For years to come, we will continue to be reminded of their lives. Their stories will live on through their loved ones and the annals of history. Periodically we hear those stories through testimonials. Next time you listen to one of these testimonials please notice something. Emphasis is never placed on the car she drove, the size of the house he owned, or the corporate position held. Ultimately, they are eulogized for the principles they stood for and the people they loved. Those are the intangibles that constitute and express a value system.

Here is the way Dr. Martin Luther expressed his value system back in the 16th century:

"I've held many things in my hands and I've lost every one of them but the things I've placed in God's hands I still possess." To be sure, our values that are based on virtues are everlasting. They are passed down from one generation to another and become part of a heritage we leave behind.

"Virtue is uniform and fixed, because she looks for approbation only from God who is the same yesterday, today and forever." (Charles Caleb Colton).

⊹ ...for the world is mine, and all that is in it.
(Psalm 50:12)


IT'S A SMALL WORLD AFTER ALL

IF YOU HAVE ever visited the Magic Kingdom at Disney World the chances are 99.9% that you have heard the song. In fact, you've heard it and then you've heard it over and over and over again.

And then, you made your way back to your hotel room. You put your head down on the pillow and the echo kept going in your head. The tune is so repetitious, so unforgettable that even after a few days have elapsed you continue to play the tune repeatedly in your head. It's a catchy tune sung by hundreds of children from all over the world. It's a simple but profound song… "It's a small, small world." It is!

The song is perhaps one of the most successful songs ever written. It is a story reminding us of the kind of world we live in. The song contains a great parable of life showing us how small our world has become and how interconnected we are! Someone's decision (good or bad) in Shook, Missouri can affect someone's life in Tokyo, Japan. I can pick up my phone at any moment and immediately place a call to a remote corner of the planet. The World Wide Web has indeed helped to create the "global village."

Since the world has become smaller and we have become so interconnected we also have become more personally responsible for how we live. A small world demands a bigger vision for the world. This vision for life and our world must be all encompassing because my decisions at the local level may have far reaching implications. To be sure, we must also remember that during all this there is a sovereign God immanently surrounding this world with his providential grace and care.

Possessing a big vision for our small world is a compelling challenge. Compelling because our times demand it and challenging because our personal vision is usually limited to our own small corner of this planet. Getting the bigger picture for our world and our role in it requires a daily effort in developing a clear vision and understanding each day. Staying updated on current events, reading literature and watching programming that enhances our understanding of the world are just some of the things we can do to broaden our perspective.

However, this is easier said than done. I must confess to you that I find myself struggling from time to time to have a progressively clearer vision for my world each day. My needs and vision tend to be more parochial. After all, I must pay my bills, fix my car and attend that next meeting. What difference will I make anyway? I'm only one person confined to a tiny space on this planet.

Well, I believe that the process of transforming our world for the better must commence at the local level as we identify areas of service that will improve our communities. It has been said that service is the rent we pay for the space we occupy. Identifying opportunities to help the less fortunate through volunteerism can and, in many instances, will rescue the disadvantaged from their plight in life. As we become more proactive locally we will identify the potential for positive change globally.

In developing my global vision, I need to know what is happening in South Africa as well as in Europe. I need to know what is happening country-wide as well as in Washington D.C. I need to keep our politicians accountable and continue to expand my horizons of knowledge. I need to give sacrificially, grow personally and be willing to change my agenda whenever necessary. The words of the late President John F. Kennedy summarize it well:

"We can help make the world safe for diversity. For in the final analysis, our most basic common link is that we all inhabit this small planet. We all breathe the same air. We all cherish our children's future. And we are all mortal." (Address at American University, 10 June 1963)

> ✢ *It is for freedom that Christ has set us free. Stand*
> *firm, then, and do not let yourselves be burdened*
> *again by a yoke of slavery.*
>
> *(Galatians 5:1)*

## HOW DO YOU SPELL FREE?

THIS MORNING I read an uncensored newspaper because we live in a country which believes in freedom of the press. This past Sunday I attended the church of my choice because this country believes and practices the free choice of religion. I am now sitting at my desk and writing down my thoughts because we believe in freedom of expression. These are just a few of the freedoms that we cherish as Americans.

Indeed, America is blessed in many ways! Tremendous natural resources, great scenic beauty, a basically robust economy and educational opportunities available to all who desire it are part of a seemingly endless list of the fruits which freedom has brought. The results of our unique 226-year-old democratic experiment seem almost supernatural. No other people in the history of mankind have achieved so much in so little time. America is unique among all nations in all recorded history! That is a powerful reality.

As I see it, there are two immediate temptations we face as a people. The first, we can take it all for granted, in which case freedom appears to be cheap. Freedom is not cheap! Freedom always has, and it always will demand a price. Our nation's various conflicts speak forcefully of the price that freedom has demanded over the years. Our present-day war on terrorism testifies to this truth and reminds us of the fragile nature of our liberties.

The second temptation is that of praising and worshiping America without recognizing the ultimate source of our unique freedoms. Ultimately, I believe that the One for whom the word "free" has a special meaning has inspired our freedom. May I offer the following acronym to remind us of where our ultimate freedom rests?

F-aith (in God)

> *Faith in God brings freedom from the bondage of the excesses of life. When we place our faith in God we are set free.*

R-eliance (on God)

> *Reliance on God brings freedom from the chains of insecurity. We can trust the Almighty to supply our strength, for God is omnipotent.*

E-nlightenment (from God)

> *Those who desire it can receive God's light. This light has been revealed to us and is available for those who truly seek it with all their hearts.*

E-ternal Life (with God)

> *Many people live in fear. They dwell on the gloomy side of life failing to recognize that God holds the future. For them, closing their eyes at the moment of death represents a frightening experience because*

*they have no vision of eternity. God will give us
freedom from fear of the future, old age and death.*

This is worth celebrating every 4th of July. It's worth a celebration!

GOD BLESS AMERICA AND GOD BLESS YOU!

⁓✛⁓ *Where there is no revelation, the people cast off
restraint; but blessed is he who keeps the law.*
*(Proverbs 29:18)*

## IN YOUR DREAMS

AND SO, THE story goes that the young missionary living in a land far, far away was daydreaming. In his daydream state he was imagining what a meeting would be like with the chief of a cannibal tribe that he would be visiting that week. He imagined asking the cannibal chief: "Do you people know anything about religion?" … and the chief answering, "Well, we got a little 'taste' of it when the last missionary came here." In your Dreams!

Do you daydream? How often do you daydream? I daydream occasionally. In fact, psychologists tell us that it is healthy to allow the imagination to take flight and construct healthy images of what life can be like. The danger of overdoing it is when daydreaming overwhelms our time and takes us outside the realm of reason or reality. But, healthy daydreaming leads us to a vision of a future that is positive, healthy, uplifting and hopeful.

Indeed, good and great leaders in history have been "dreamers." They have been visionary in seeing their role in life and God's place in that vision. Who can deny the transforming power of Dr. Martin Luther King's vision? His famous "I have a dream" speech on the steps of the Lincoln Memorial has become part of our national collective conscience. Our lives have been changed for the better because of his singular vision. It was a "dream" enveloped by God's direction for a people. It also merits noting that those who dare to dream the good and great dreams must also be willing to make personal sacrifices in realizing their vision.

A sure mark of a good leader is the ability to distinguish between unrealistic daydreaming and those dreams/ visions that can become reality for the good of all. This takes wisdom and it takes work. Our pluralistic society cherishes those leaders in government, church and the military that strive to achieve unity amid diversity. Indeed, America is no longer a "melting pot" but rather, it is more like a mosaic of cultures, ethnicities and language groups that have come to our blessed nation to realize their good dreams. Those leaders who understand that uniting all these diverse groups is not only worthy but also attainable, will affect the most positive outcomes. By contrast, those who allow division and disunity will contribute to a growing sense of factionalism and discord.

For a moment, just think of the great potential we will realize as a nation as we continue to unify people from all backgrounds who contribute their talents and diversity into our national mix. We can and will become a model to those nations that struggle with internal division (and in many cases violence) due to racial, ethnic and religious tensions.

The dream of finding unity in our diversity can only become reality as we apply it individually. To be sure, we need leaders that endorse this vision, but we must individually choose to apply it. The testing ground for the application of this national distinctive is not down the street. It is in each person that the dream is fleshed out.

For instance, do we go out of our way to socialize with people of another ethnic/cultural group? Can we claim to have good friends that originate from another language group? Do we attend cultural events that will expose us to people from other countries who reside here? These things unlock the door to experience personal growth and enrichment. Those of us who embrace and celebrate our diversity will become instruments of unity.

America is the nation of my dreams. In the nation of my dreams there is no room for division. There can't be! As we look around us, what do we see? We can see the vast richness and tremendous potential stored up in each person regardless of race, language, culture, gender and religion. In fact, I will go as far as stating that creating division is the equivalent of despising our nation and dishonoring God. To be sure, there is no room for divisions in our great nation.

Great works in great nations start with a dream. It is a dream founded and planted on a godly vision for a people. It is a vision of achieving unity in the midst of diversity. It is a vision that can give us a taste of heaven.

·✢· *After that, he poured water into a basin and began to wash his disciples' feet, drying them with the towel that was wrapped around him.*
*(John 13:5)*

## To Lead is to Serve

"What do you want to be when you grow up?" Do you remember that question? Some of us may still be trying to formulate the answer. It is a favorite question we periodically ask our kids. The answers our children give are usually, "Policeman, fireman, nurse." Some children get visionary and may say, "movie star, singer, doctor, ball player," and maybe even… "a chaplain." One imaginative six-year old responded as follows: "when I grow up I want to be either a car mechanic or a garbage collector." When asked as to why he quickly said, "So I can get dirty!"

Let's have some fun! Let us take that same question and ask it another way. Just for a moment, let's imagine asking God what he wants us to be when we grow up. Suddenly it is a whole new question. I suspect that God's answer may be something like this, "I want you to be different. I want you to serve others. I want you to be a helper." Why? Because genuine service to others expresses concern, generosity and elevates our spirit to new levels of personal maturity.

However, I cannot recall the number of times that people have readily offered the following response, "I want to be a servant." I believe that culturally we are discouraged to be servants. To our ear it may sound unimportant to be a servant. Our culture tends to measure success in terms of titles, duties and tasks. Our titles generally describe who we are. Our culture has created a hierarchy of duties and at the bottom of the totem pole is the title "servant." I suspect that while most of us know that we will never be the greatest, we sure don't want to be the least. I also suspect that most of us would rather give an order than wear a servant's apron. Yes, there exists an inherent tension in practicing servanthood. Where do I draw the line between servanthood and slavery or humility and self worth? Where is the boundary that separates my rights from others' rights?

Indeed, I sense we need a renewed understanding of what it means to be a servant. I propose that if we aspire to lead we must be prepared to serve others. Its corollary is that genuine service will qualify us to lead with integrity. Therefore, in renewing and defining our understanding of leadership we need to identify its principle, its profile and its promise.

The principle of servant leadership: This principle dictates that we cannot exercise effective leadership until we are postured to serve others. This means that mission accomplishment is meaningless if we are not taking care of others. The servant leader seeks to meet goals and see to the needs of others. Both tasks need to be accomplished simultaneously. Servant leadership is practiced both at work and at home.

The profile of the servant: The profile is exemplified through those little things that express encouragement and concern. It is in sending a greeting card, making that special phone call or sending the impromptu email. It consists in those acts of self-sacrifice for the sake of another.

The promise of service: Its promise is realized in selfless personal fulfillment and self-realization as a person identifies with the will of God for his creation. His/her satisfaction comes from knowing that he/she has made a difference in another's life.

There's a denomination of Baptists known as Primitive Baptists. Among some of their traditions is a very distinctive practice of "foot washings." That is, at one point in their worship service they wash each other's feet. Not only do they have the cleanest feet in Christendom, but also, they do it as a cogent reminder of servanthood.

Indeed, to be a servant requires courage, humility and genuine concern. True service doesn't distinguish big from small opportunities. True service delights in God's approval.

⬩✝⬩ *For even when we were with you, we gave you this rule: If a man will not work, he shall not eat.*
*(2 Thessalonians 3:10)*

## Why Work, Anyway?

HEY, WHY DO people work anyway? An obvious answer can be: to survive. Work will bring the funds and the benefits that provide for a standard of living. Another view as to why we work has been expressed in a popular bumper sticker that reads: "I owe, I owe/ so off to work I go." Many perceive work to be just that – a way to pay off the mountain of debts. Yet for others work is seen as mere necessity – empty of any pleasure or sense of fulfillment. For those in this dilemma work becomes devoid of any sense of excitement, purpose or vision for the future. "Drudgery" becomes a good way to describe work under these circumstances.

But let's face it. The work we do is important. We spend most of our time at work. We will spend more time socializing with co-workers than with some of our own family members. And remember: work is here to stay!

So, what I feel is needed during this Labor Day weekend is a serious reevaluation of our attitudes about "work." That is, let's have a "vision adjustment." Careful contemplation over the value and purpose for work could provide us with a healthier attitude and change the way we live our lives.

Work provides us the opportunity to be responsible. This clearly implies that stealing from an employer is not justifiable under any conditions. An honest and responsible attitude will instill rightness about our work. Through work we provide for our needs, develop skills, and contribute to the community where we live. To work in a career that benefits others or at which you are skillful will bring a sense of satisfaction and self-esteem.

Work affords us the opportunity to help others. Often taken for granted, this opportunity is life fulfilling and enriching. Through our income we can be in a position to help the less fortunate in our society. Living in an economic environment that worships the "living-on-credit" ethic renders this opportunity difficult to achieve. Therefore, using our work to help others may require that we put our work responsibilities in a different perspective. When seeing it from this point of view, work can then become more of a "sacred" opportunity than a necessary drudgery. Our work can become truly significant when we view it in terms of a "calling" in life. Seen from this perspective, we may even approach our work with some sense of reverence because we've been placed there with a great purpose.

As we examine these reasons for our work, we will discover that what we do for a living can have a positive impact on the lives of people around us. It should challenge us to be responsible about what we do for a living. At the forefront of the work ethic is to see our job as the task that God has entrusted to us, and to accomplish it in that spirit, allowing ourselves to be guided by the Almighty. The valuable thing is to perceive our job, as well as our other activities, as an adventure directed by God himself.

I close with a quote from Dorothy L Sayers:

"I ask that work should be looked upon, not as a necessary drudgery...but as a way of life in which the nature of man should find its proper exercise and delight and so fulfill itself to the glory of God."

> ⊹ *Where can I go from your Spirit? Where can I flee from your presence? If I rise on the wings of the dawn, if I settle on the far side of the sea, even there your hand will guide me, your right hand will hold me fast.*
>
> *(Psalm 139:7, 9-10)*

## DO WE DARE ASK? (ON BIGOTRY)

BACK IN THE 1970's "All in the Family" was the leading situation comedy in the nation. The program flourished in the wake of the Civil Rights Movement. You can still see reruns on television. Archie Bunker was its main protagonist and America laughed at all his flaws, his narrow-mindedness and arrogance. We laughed at his irrational sense of logic and America laughed and cried at the man's bigotry and prejudice. Archie Bunker had created his own reality. It was a reality created in his image.

In one of the episodes George Jefferson, his African-American neighbor, drops by to visit. George was a man equally prejudiced and he and Archie started to talk about God. Archie Bunker goes into an explanation as to why he believes that God is a white man. In his own peculiar logic Bunker creates the following syllogism: "Man is made in the image of God. Archie is a white man. Therefore, God must be white." Archie expounds: "Besides, all the pictures of God I've seen, all the pictures of Jesus I've seen always show him as a white man." George Jefferson quickly responds, "Bunker, you were looking at the pictures' negatives."

All in The Family vividly demonstrated that there is a very thin line between comedy and drama. After all, it was sad to observe that both Archie and his African-American counterpart had created their own notion of God. The blight of bigotry does that. It creates a god molded in the image of the bigot.

In celebrating Martin Luther King Day, we may dare to use the time for personal introspection. We may dare to ask ourselves the difficult questions as we honor the life of a man who dared to ask the tough questions. Indeed, Dr. King gave his full measure of devotion in challenging an entire society to examine, challenge and transform their preconceived realities.

What happens when we dare to fit God into our own little box? What happens when we dare to create God in our image? What happens when we dare to give God his marching orders? Do we dare ask ourselves the tough questions? Is there still, in the deepest recesses of our hearts, the slightest hint of bigotry? To be sure, all of us deal with personal bias at some level. What I'm addressing here is the type of bias that stifles my opportunity to relate with all people across the ethnic and cultural spectrum. I would submit that this is an important key to our national cohesion and world peace in the 21st century.

I have found that ultimately our struggles with interethnic bias can often be traced to unresolved struggles with God; for if God is love then truly God loves all people of all races. As we fail to experience this unconditional love of the Almighty in our own lives, we will fail to reach others with the compassionate and transparent love of God. When "God's will be done" becomes "my will be done," we are daring to limit the power of God in our lives by creating a God that will fit a personal agenda. Please be assured of this that God is everywhere and knows the deepest secrets of our hearts. We cannot be fugitives from God no more than we can stop being who we are, for *"Where can I go from your spirit? Where can I flee from your presence?"* God's unrelenting passion is for people, all people. Dr. Martin Luther King, Jr. knew this and was compelled to lead a transformative movement. The genius of the Civil Rights Movement is that it has never truly ended. It continues to ask the tough questions. I truly believe that our vision for the rights of all people can be as great as our belief in the power of God to transform and shape our hearts.

"If any of you are around when I have to meet my day, … I'd like for somebody to mention that day that Martin Luther King, Jr. tried to give his life serving others… tried to feed the hungry… clothe those who were naked… tried to love and serve humanity." (Ebenezer Baptist Church, 4 Feb 1968)

⚜ *Everyone must submit himself to the governing authorities, for there is no authority except that which God has established.*

*(Romans 13:1)*

## THE MULE WON THE RACE (ON VOTING)

IT IS A true story. In 1883 in the city of Allentown, New Jersey a "wooden Indian," the kind you find in front of cigar stores, was placed on the ballot for Justice of the Peace. The wooden Indian was registered under the false name of Abner Robbins. When the ballots were counted, Abner won over the incumbent Justice by seven votes. Here is another true story somewhat like the first but more recent. It happened in 1938. The name of Boston Curtis appeared on the ballot for Republican Committeeman from Wilton, Washington. However, there was only one problem. Boston Curtis was the name of a mule. The town's Mayor had sponsored the animal to demonstrate that people knew very little about the candidates. The Mayor proved his point and the mule won the race.

Indeed, too many voting citizens seldom take the time to really investigate a political candidate's qualifications to govern effectively. Have we taken the time to investigate a candidate's moral standards, voting records, political philosophy and positions on other important issues? Grant it, some of us may suffer from a sense of disillusionment with politics. However, this does not excuse us from disengaging from a democratic privilege as vital as voting. To be sure, men and women in uniform are presently sacrificing life and limb to ensure that this privilege does not go away. This being the case, we are called to participate integrally in the process of selecting the next leader of the free world.

Please, do not worry. I will not tell you whom to vote for. I will not insult your intelligence nor violate my responsibility in that fashion. But, if you are a person of faith I'm sure you will agree that there isn't an area of life that is left untouched or unaddressed by our spiritual beliefs. You see, people of faith also bear a responsibility as to the way we engage in the political process.

Let me illustrate. My Christian faith teaches me that the governmental authorities that exist are part of God's plan for maintaining good order and stability in society. The Bible goes as far as calling governmental authorities "God's servants/ministers" (Bible, Romans 13:4) The principle, the concept of authority informs me that the living God is the ultimate authority and that God has expressed that authority in different ways. Governments are called and formed to serve a purpose and that purpose is fulfilled within the context of authority. Therefore, the government's authority is a delegated authority from the Most High. The purpose of authority, then, is to promote the good and to hold evil acts in check through an equitable judicial system. So, the purpose of governmental authority is to work out part of God's providential care amid society.

Consequently, as a person of faith, I bear certain responsibilities in that relationship that I must take seriously. This would include, but is not limited to, my responsibility in choosing the next President of The Republic. After all, this is the person that will make decisions impacting war and peace as well as economic policies affecting our personal finances.

However, let me take this up one more level. For I submit that my involvement in the political process is a sacred responsibility. It represents for me an opportunity to be partners with God in selecting those who would govern with good order, stability and justice. On the other side of that coin I also bear the responsibility to use all legal means available to remove from office those authorities that have violated their sacred trust. Now, all this electing and governing takes place within an imperfect society with imperfect people and from time to time we will be disappointed by the frailties of our elected officials. In those moments I am reminded that "it is better to trust in the Lord than to put confidence in man" (Psalm 118:8). Nonetheless, as Americans we share in the best system devised for maintaining good order, stability and justice.

By the way, I suspect that the good Lord is neither a registered Democrat nor Republican. I think that He may just be an independent. Don't forget to vote!

# SECTION XI
## HOLIDAYS-HOLYDAYS

*When your words came, I ate them; they were my joy and my heart's delight, for I bear your name, O LORD God Almighty.*

*(Jeremiah 15:16)*

## FOOD FOR THOUGHT (ON NEW YEAR)

To THIS DAY I dread having to eat seeded grapes. Just the thought of it repels me. Allow me to explain because this comes from a childhood trauma. You see in my family we upheld a tradition that had been passed down to us from Spain. It was an ancient tradition that could be traced back hundreds of years.

Every New Year's Eve all those present at the party were given twelve (12) individual grapes. As the clock approached midnight we had about two minutes to devour the grapes. Not ten (10) grapes. No, not eleven (11) but all twelve (12) grapes! It was done for good luck during the coming twelve months. The superstition was that if you didn't eat all the grapes you would probably get the plague and die. Herein lays the genesis of my problem. The grapes had pits! Just the thought of having to deal with the pits ruined my New Year's celebration.

It is interesting how different cultures have this tradition in some form. In the United States some will eat black-eyed peas or cabbage or herring with honey. Others may eat sardines and salt for good luck in the coming year. The Japanese eat long noodles. The Greeks bake special breads. Anthropologists say that eating certain foods for good luck in the coming year dates to the ancient Babylonian Empire. Still, of all the fruits available on the planet, why the Spaniards ever selected grapes with pits for good luck is beyond me!

Well, you know what is said about "good luck": Good luck is the residue of hard work. While some may wish for good luck in the current year, I believe that we should be looking for a firmer substance to stand on. I believe that we should look for substantial nutrition that will provide us with the "inner substance" for successfully facing the road ahead in any year.

In my New Year's preparations, I've eliminated the tradition passed down to me from the ancient Spaniards (thank God) and I've resolved to keep some resolutions worthy of realizing. I've understood that my past failures in keeping resolutions have been due to a lack of focus and an over abundance of negligence on my part. I've allowed myself to become distracted by other less important items and the things that have been really important have not received the attention they merit. So here is a primer on lifelong resolutions that have given me some food for thought.

1. LEAVE A LEGACY: We often associate the passing of a personal legacy with material riches or a family heirloom. The legacy I refer to here is much more valuable, however. It is the legacy of a good name. The concept is very simple. Our name will outlive us long after we are gone from the scene. Our good name will reveal to others who we are because our reputation will go "before" us.

Leaving a legacy will engage us in the lives of others, especially the young. As we mentor the young, be it our children or other young people, we will encourage them to be the very best that they can be. Leaving a good legacy also means that we keep promises made. In the coming year let us do all we can to make life just a little sweeter for those we come in contact with.

2. GIVE GIFTS THAT LAST: These gifts would include,…the gift of caring…as we express concern for those in need…as we express affection for family and friends that we have been blessed with.

How about the gift of a smile, for it takes less facial muscles to smile than it takes to frown.

Also, give away some encouragement. So many times, all it takes is a simple expression of affirmation to lift the spirit of the downcast. To encourage means to empower.

3. KEEP ALERT AND STAND FIRM: Part of the adventure of living is that we never know what circumstances may demand our immediate attention and decision. Let us be quick to show good judgment and to use our heads as well as our hearts in making good decisions.

So here is some food for thought that has kept me thinking for the last few days. If you must eat grapes for good luck, make sure that they are the pit-less variety.

⁘ *I will give thanks to the LORD because of his righteousness and will sing praise to the name of the LORD Most High.*

*(Psalm 7:17)*

## "Thanks-Living"/ Thanksgiving

A CERTAIN LADY went to visit her friend and took her six-year-old son Johnny along. Upon arriving at the house, the boy started to complain that he was hungry. The friend offered Johnny an orange. Immediately after the lady offered him the orange Johnny's mother said to him: "Now what do you say, Johnny?" Johnny looked at the orange, handed it back to the gracious lady and said: "Peel it." Well, this is hardly an expression of "thanksgiving."

Unfortunately, so many of us take the gifts life brings us for granted. Like Johnny we may not do well at being thankful. Thanksgiving, or should I say "thanks-living" (living with an attitude of gratitude) is important if we are to enjoy the fullness of life. Possessing an ever-greater ability to appreciate what we already have is an even greater challenge in our day and time. We may never be truly satisfied with the gifts we already have.

For the Thanksgiving holiday I would like to express some thoughts about proper gratitude, or better yet, how to maintain an attitude of "thanks-living" in our lives that will carry us beyond this most unique American of holidays.

Let's begin with the following truism: "thanksgiving is an attitude." An attitude is a behavior. Because it is a personal behavior we do exert a high degree of control over it. The Thanksgiving Holiday invites us to participate in this spirit of inner gratitude. It is an "attitude of gratitude" that can teach us so much about balanced living because there truly is so much to be thankful for... everyday. This lifestyle or "thanks-living" can pervade all of life and make an important contribution to the way we live all of life. How can this be?

Well, first, living thankfully is not the same as being "happy" all the time. Happiness is a feeling. Happiness is a response to an experience. Thankful living ("thanks-living) is a behavior based on a decision of my will. This decision is grounded on the unchanging reality that life itself is a gift and worthy of fruitful living. I have discovered that it is further based on the truth that God has given me a life to experience in all its abundance, in all its vitality. What's the practical translation of all this?

1. If I've smashed my thumb with a hammer, I still have the rest of my fingers.
2. If I've been in a car accident, it could've been a lot worse.
3. If the Redskins lose again, well, they can't get any worse (I'm in trouble now).

To be sure, the foundation, the reality of "thanks-living" is founded on the objective,
palpable fact that the life we live and breathe is precious because it is a gift from the Almighty. Therefore, "thanks-living" is an elevation of the heart.

Do we go through the motions of living (as though we're the walking dead) or do we live with a sense of the presence of God? This "behavior" is a choice. It is always a choice.

This path of gratitude isn't easy but it's worth the effort. See what there is to be thankful for rather than dwelling on the negative things. Some of you already have this attitude of "thanks-living." It is an attitude that encourages and inspires others.

So, in preparation for this national holiday which is so distinctly American in its culture, let us use this time to remember that "thanks-living" is a life-long calling.

⁘ *This will be a sign to you: You will find a baby wrapped in cloths and lying in a manger.*
*(Luke 2:12)*

## SHOPPING MALL SYNDROME (PRE CHRISTMAS)

"JOY TO THE World," the name of that hymn loved by many can be easily forgotten during the Christmas season as our thinking and our time become dominated by that most dreaded Christmas disease known as "the shopping mall syndrome." The initial symptoms are very subtle and hardly recognizable. It usually starts when we sit down to write the list of those who will be at the receiving end of our generosity. The motives are good but as we develop the list the issues become more complex.

You know what I mean:

- What if Aunt Harriet shows up with a gift this year and I don't have one for her?

- What is the politically correct gift to give my boss this year?

- If I do not get my child the GI Joe with the Kung-Fu grip he'll be traumatized for life!

As the days and the weeks progress the symptoms become more pronounced.

You finally hit rock bottom when you break out in a cold sweat next to the "Barbie Doll" section of the toy store. You realize that you have overdrawn your checking account by $500.00 and you need to cover it with a cash advance "pronto." At this point "Joy to the World" has turned into a new tune, "The Christmas Time Blues."

Don't take me wrong! Christmas time is all about giving and receiving. However, "the shopping mall syndrome" does create confusion in people's minds about the motives and the reasons for the giving. So, to redirect our motives and our methods we need to return to the original Christmas story, commemorated each year. As we return to the "manger" at Bethlehem we can relearn some vital realities about present-day Christmas. The historical birth of the "Christ" child in very humble surroundings points us to some very simple and very practical verities:

- YOU CAN'T BUY CHRISTMAS; YOU CAN ONLY GIVE IT. The very first Christmas, the birth of Jesus, had nothing to do with purchased gifts but it had everything to do with passion for persons. The holiday season reminds us that God's passion is for people. Our exchange of gifts is symbolic of God's gift to humankind, that is, God's incomparable gift.

- YOU CAN'T BUY CHRISTMAS; YOU CAN ONLY BELIEVE IN IT. Christmas represents our saying "yes" to something beyond all emotions and feelings. It believes in God's possibilities to overcome my impossibilities. When you give a gift, it is your expression of "belief"; it is your expression of faith and acknowledgement of the season's significance.

- YOU CAN'T BUY CHRISTMAS; YOU CAN ONLY
  LIVE IT EVERYDAY! I believe that our lives
  would be revolutionized if we truly understood and practiced the belief that each day
  is a precious gift. Indeed, to live like this
  would become a daily celebration of life
  itself. "Whoever lives by the truth comes
  into the light so that what has been done
  has been done through God." (John 3:21)

Allow simplicity and sincerity to be your guiding principles at
Christmas.

"Joy to the World!"

⊹ *Thanks be to God for his indescribable gift!*
*(2 Corinthians 9:15)*

## GIFTS THAT WILL LAST (ON CHRISTMAS)

IN MY LAST article I attempted to warn you of the dangers related
to "the shopping mall syndrome." I tried to point out that if you
are not careful, the "Christmas Times Blues" could grip your spirit
of giving in a vise through unnecessary overspending. The advice
was given with a view towards maintaining simplicity and sincerity as the guiding principles for the Christmas season. The advice
was also given towards preventing the typical emotional overload, verging on nervous breakdown, which will turn you into a
"scrooge" very easily.

So, if you did things right, if you listened to the chaplain, your
shopping worries are over. Right now, you're unstressed. You will

fill out and mail your Christmas cards with plenty of anticipation. You will purchase and wrap the gifts and place them under the Christmas tree and you will have done it all debt free! What a joy! It will give you time to contemplate over your accomplishment.

For instance, what superlative expressions would describe the Christmas gifts you purchase? What flowery adjectives will you use in describing your delight over the gifts you will give in the holiday season. To be sure, the use of such words as "fabulous," "fantastic," "splendid," etc. can reach an all time high in our vocabulary in describing gifts we give and those we receive. But beware! Professors of communication encourage their students to avoid the overuse of superlatives ("outstanding" … etc.). Their advice is that these types of words should be used infrequently and only when necessary. Overuse of superlatives is usually a sign of exaggeration and superficiality.

I do hope that as discriminating and astute shoppers we have selected gifts that will communicate the "Three Essentials" of the holiday season: personal, practical, pleasant

May your gift be PERSONAL… for Christmas celebrates a most personal of gifts which the Almighty gave to the world in the person of a child. This child developed in humble surroundings and in time his teachings and personal example gave humanity a new perspective on how to relate to God. Indeed, we can make the claim that his impact has changed many countless lives for the better. His impact changed the history of the world.

Application: Know the recipient of your gift. Be aware of the person's needs and respond to that need with a gift that matches your pocketbook and your recipient's need.

May your gift be PRACTICAL…for the message of Christmas is practical for the present and most definitely for the future. "Peace on earth, good will towards man" is not pie in the sky. This message is good and practical for the here and now. It is good for all seasons.

Application: be practical in your selection of the gift. A gift that will last has frequent use to solve practical needs. Its practical use will be a reminder of your concern and appreciation

May your gift be PLEASANT...for God's most pleasant gift was given with love and sacrifice. The Christmas story relates that this gift cost heaven the very best it had to offer.

Application: your pleasant gift will bring smiles long after the holiday season is over. It will act as a soothing and pleasant reminder that life, with all its complexities, is a pleasant journey after all.

Thank you, Lord,! ... for your superlative gift!

⁀⊕⁀ *Glory to God in the highest, and on earth peace to men on whom his favor rests.*

*(Luke 2:14)*

## PEACE?...ON EARTH? (POST CHRISTMAS)

IT WAS THE Sunday before Christmas and a precocious four-year-old boy, attending his Sunday school class, told his teacher, "There are some poor kids next to us who have no daddy, no toys and no Aunt Jane." The young Sunday school teacher immediately felt that she had identified a teachable moment. She seized the opportunity and asked the boy, "Wouldn't you like to give them something?" "Yes" he answered. "I'd like to give them Aunt Jane!"

Let me give you some background. In this case, Aunt Jane was viewed by the family as a first cousin to Sadam Hussein. When she came every Christmas, she would hold the family hostage (i.e., better buy her a gift above a certain dollar amount, or else...). Aunt

Jane possessed an insufferable attitude and was just an all-around difficult person to deal with.

Hey, do you have an "Aunt Jane" type of person in your life? These are people that may sing the angel's son but have never been confused for an angel. Sometimes we find them at our jobs, our homes, our churches or even... in our mirror.

In the season that sings about the hope of peace, the "aunt Jane'" types only hints at the remote possibility of peace, of the personal kind. These are the "difficult people" we encounter in life. They are not ambassadors of peace. Are you an ambassador of peace? Am I?

The original Christmas account narrates the prophesied birth of a special child. The biblical passages highlight the appearance of angelic ambassadors announcing the child's birth and the dawning of a new era: "...and on earth- peace to men on whom his favor rests."

Well, the greatest message of Christmas is still the promise of peace! Few other words in the language of humanity fill the heart with greater desire for total, complete, lasting and everlasting tranquility than the word "peace." At the time of this special child's birth there existed tyranny, oppression, and human indignity. It was a violent world where children were abused, and domestic violence was known to occur. However, have times really changed? The need for peace today is no less compelling. To be sure, we moderns have developed some rather ingenious capabilities for killing each other.

As we see violence in our world, we are justified in questioning the new era of world peace that "the Christ child" would usher in. Well, the key to this is one of interpretation. Here's my perspective:

I would love to superimpose God's peace plan on the Middle East, the streets of Baghdad and in the life of tyrants. I would like to wave the magic wand and make it happen. However, I know that I cannot. Nevertheless, I can do something about the "aunt Jane" personality in me. You can do something about the "Dr. Jekyll and Mr. Hyde" personality in you. God's peace plan must first be intensely personal before it can be outwardly contagious. God's peace plan must reign in each person's life individually.

"And on earth – peace to men on whom his favor rest." You know, I like the sound of that. It's comforting. It sounds noble. It sounds like something I'd like to have but there is a catch. You see this kind of peace is supernatural, otherworldly and downright godly. Therefore, "peace to men" can only be the by-product of a "relationship" with God. This inner peace is not dependent on an attitude adjustment, electroshock therapy or esoteric mind control techniques. This "peace to men" is not even the result of good intentions. Rather, this inner, abiding, personal, supernatural peace can only be derived through a surrender of the inner self to the power of God to transform us. Attitude change and good intentions become the by-products of personal transformation.

Before I can live peaceably with anyone I must first be at peace with myself. The challenge of Christmas is making peace of the personal kind…, which begins as we, individually, make peace with God. PEACE!

·✦· *All go to the same place; all come from dust, and to dust all return.*

*(Ecclesiastes 3:20)*

## FROM DUST TO DUST (ON ASH WEDNESDAY)

"FROM DUST YOU have come. To dust you shall return." It is a sobering statement to say the least. This declaration will be repeated countless millions of times once a year as people from various

Christian denominations around the world receive a peculiar mark on their foreheads made with ashes. The ashes are burnt palm leaves and are dispensed by ministers who will utter a peculiar phrase each time the ashes (in the form of a cross) are placed on each forehead. Ash Wednesday marks the beginning of a special time in the Christian church's calendar known as "Lent."

Lent is a period of forty days that ends on Palm Sunday which marks the beginning of Passion Week, culminating on Easter Sunday. Many of the faithful observe the season of Lent with fasting and other spiritual disciplines. While not all Christian denominations observe Ash Wednesday, all of Christendom does observe Lent. While my Christian tradition does not observe Ash Wednesday, I would like to refocus on the ashes nonetheless because I believe there's something in it for all of us.

The ashes are a reminder to all humanity of our inner vulnerability and weakness before the presence of an awesome God. It reminds me that I am not invincible and that I am, in fact, a broken vessel before the presence of the Almighty. Precisely because of this ultimate helplessness I need God. Because one day the tent will collapse, I need God.

In these days of high technology, busy lives and complex schedules it is important to take pause and be reminded of our own vulnerability. Indeed, Ash Wednesday and the Lenten season can give us enough pause to realize that I am not indispensable, after all, and that the world will continue to turn, and my job will still be there when I get back to it. Ash Wednesday and the Lenten season can give us just enough hiatus to celebrate the richness of God's grace. For if from the dust I have come and to dust I will return, then tomorrow is never promised to me and the life I have today is by the grace of God. That is what Ash Wednesday is mostly about: God's provision of grace. How can we try to understand this grace?

Well, my wife Vicky has told me about her childhood visit to Niagara Falls. I've never been there. She remembers experiencing a majestic sense of awe. She can still recall the fall's deafening sound and it's overpowering, unending activity. Imagine 200,000 tons of water per minute plunging down twelve stories into the Niagara River. The Almighty could have used a lot less water. God did not. God could have made the falls lower, but he did not. However, Because of its unique design people are drawn to it.

What a picture of God's grace! It is limitless, unending, awe-in-spiring, deafening in its majesty and overpowering in its love. People are drawn to it by its power and surprised by its simplicity.

So, it is very possible that one could catch a glimpse or even experience the grace of God through the reality of our personal vulnerability. God delights in revealing himself to those who long to experience his grace and are humble enough to express that need.

·✛· *All the prophets testify about him that everyone who believes in him receives forgiveness of sins through his name.*

*(Acts 10:43)*

## THE GOSPEL OF THE SECOND CHANCE (ON EASTER)

WHAT DOES EASTER mean to you? It can mean many different things to a variety of people. To be sure, like so many other holidays, Easter has taken on a commercial flavor in our culture. The seasonal marketing of the ubiquitous Easter Bunny increases the profit margin for many retail shops. Easter fashions mark the change-over from winter to spring and the all-important Easter-egg hunt brings smiles to the faces of countless children. As Easter ushers in the season of spring it brings a sense of freshness and renewal that inspires many to reaffirm the goodness of life itself.

However, Easter, in its very essence, is a spiritual expression born in an historical event so magnificent in its nature that to this day challenges the imagination and faith of numerous people. Indeed, to believe in Easter is to believe in life itself. The Easter story and its claim of resurrected life is God's way of saying "I forgive you." If the historical claim of Easter is true, and I believe it is, then it shows me how far God is willing to go to extend his forgiveness and grant me peace of mind about the future. Easter is God's great and definitive statement that the Almighty has offered us a second chance at life, (of the temporal and eternal variety). This reality is beautifully illustrated in the biblical account of the very first Easter. It is a most human story about friendship, betrayal, forgiveness and renewal. Its two principal players are Jesus of Nazareth and Simon Peter, Jesus' most stalwart follower. In Simon Peter we may see a character that we can identify with. He will touch our hearts with his very human qualities. Known for his bold, outspoken and courageous nature, Peter possessed great potential for greatness. More than once, he promised never to disown his master and leader. Yet, when the moment of truth came, not only did he disown Jesus once, but he denied him three times. Wanting to save his own neck, he personally betrayed a most cherished friendship. Finally realizing the depravity of his act, Simon Peter begins to weep bitterly. They were tears of sorrow and regret overflowing from the deepest crevices of his soul.

I don't know about you, but I can identify with this man. I can identify with this struggle of faith and loyalty to the things of God. But, I too am prepared and open to embrace God's unconditional offer for a second chance. The miracle of the resurrected life is

God's way of saying "I'm here for you!" It is God's way of giving us a hand and inviting us to personal renewal and hope. I must admit that as an ordained minister I tend to expect too much of Easter. After all, it is Easter! My expectation is to see every single heart captured by the power of God's eternal source of power for living. Yes, I am confident that we can expect a great deal out of Easter. I believe that God wants us to!

I guarantee you that we are not expecting too much out of Easter if we ask God to help us overcome all that is hindering our lives. The gospel of the second chance restored a man broken and despairing over his personal act of betrayal. Simon Peter embraced God's offer of forgiveness and restoration and his life was changed. I submit that it is not too much to expect the same miracle for us. Surely, nothing, nothing is impossible with God!!

The gospel of the second chance teaches me that there is no rock so deep that I can't move it (with God's help). That is, I can change for the better. I can start life over. The Easter story reminds me that there is no dream so lost that I can't get it back. God is the rebuilder of broken dreams. While life may have dealt me a bad hand I just need to hang in long enough to experience the restorative power of God's grace. Don't give up! The Easter account informs me that there's no pain so great that I can't endure it. I do not know much about pain, but I have had some experiences. In retrospect I have learned that when life is at its worst, God has put an invisible net under me. I have found myself standing when I would rather run. God's unrelenting promise has been to give me what I need to get through the experience.

So, Easter is the day to be renewed and be rebuilt (inside and out) by God's resurrection power. This is the day that the Lord has made. Happy Easter!

# SECTION XII
## THE FUTURE IS NOW!

 *Brothers, I do not consider myself yet to have taken hold of it. But one thing I do: Forgetting what is behind and straining toward what is ahead...*
                                        *(Philippians 3:13)*

NEW BEGINNINGS

"FORGETTING THOSE THINGS which are behind...' I press toward the goal."

THE MONTH OF January is named after Janus, The Roman God of beginnings,

> *Custodian of the universe, the guardian of gates and doors. He held sacred the first hour of the day, first day of the month, and first month of the year (which bears his name).*

Indeed! Much can be said about new beginnings and the opportunity it presents for starting afresh and recommitting oneself to those beliefs and deep convictions that drive our individual lives. This is the kind of opportunity I am presented with as a minister and chaplain to many.

By way of introduction, I could load up this article with personal biographical facts that would not be all that exciting to read.

For beginners, I think it is important for you to know something about what is driving my motivation currently. You need to know something about my immediate focus and the desires of my heart. I believe that this kind of information is much more important than details and data that would otherwise cover this page and stretch your patience.

A diversity of ministry venues and opportunities cover the landscape of my journey. As I've arrived to serve at these different venues, unforeseen challenges would lay before me and new goals awaited their attainment. More than anything I always desired that each new tenure bring renewal in my life and to the life of those I served, with God's help.

With a forward look, I always desired to move ahead with the hope and certainty that the answer to many of life's challenges lies in a proper understanding and application of the word "RELATIONSHIP."

- A proper RELATIONSHIP with God. – For God is the One creator and sustainer of all. That relationship is realized and sustained in proper and focused worship.

- A proper RELATIONSHIP with my family. – For the family is God-ordained and is the basis for good education, good morals and good continuity in life.

- A proper RELATIONSHIP with friends and those that I have and presently serve…as I understand that there is no such thing as a perfect human being. Reconciliation, forgiveness and encouragement are the order of the day when it comes to friendships and relationship building.

As I press toward new goals and attempt to envision what the Almighty may have in store for me, I am filled with anticipation and nervous excitement. I am reminded that once you take your eyes off the goal your mind may stay fixed on what's in the past. Championship track stars will testify to this truth asserting that to win the race you must keep your eyes on the finish line. If you look to the sides or to the back, you'll slow down and lose the race.

So, let us stop looking back. Let us learn from the mistakes of the past rather than dwell over them. Instead, let us put ourselves in proper Relationship and watch how the future marvelously unfolds before us.

The US Navy's Chaplain Corp's Vision Statement is as follows:

*Devoted to God and country, we will unite to deliver innovative, life-transforming service throughout and beyond the Sea Services.*

I seek with all my heart to fulfill this universal vision of the Chaplain Corps to the best of my ability and truly anticipate God's protection and richest blessings as I lean towards the future, with God's help!

✟ *Jesus Christ is the same yesterday and today and forever.*

*(Hebrews 13:8)*

## CHANGE IS FOREVER

WOULD YOU AGREE that we live in a changing world? According to Heraclites, the ancient Greek philosopher, "you can't step into the same river twice." Think about it. Just when we think that we have things figured out, something happens to make us change. Just when we think that we have it "nailed down," it's time to change again. If there is anything in this material world which is unchanging is "change" itself.

How do we respond to change? Do we have a love-hate relationship with change? On the one hand, we can resist and even repel the mere thought of change. On the other hand, we know that without change there is just no progress at all.

When we look towards the future we can adopt one of three perspectives. First, we can anticipate that the future will not be an extension of the past. Second, the future may not turn out to be what we think it will be. Third, change will continue to accelerate at a more rapid pace. That third possibility can be scary. Many people will reject and resist the inevitability of change, but a few others will accept change and even celebrate the new possibilities that change brings about. In fact, the following is a change index that will gauge your adaptability to "change." Give yourself 10 points for "yes" and 0 points for "no."

1. Have you changed your hairstyle in the past five years?

2. Do you enjoy trying foods you have never tried before?

3. Do you enjoy making new friends?

4. Have you voted for someone other than your political party in the last ten years?

5. Have you switched your clothing style in the last five years?

6. Do you find the prospect of a job change exciting?

7. Would you consider visiting a church of a different denomination?

8. Do you welcome new and innovative ways of doing your job?

9. How traumatic is the thought of relocating to a new town?

10. Can you hum the tune or sing the song of any popular song written in the last year?

So, how changeable are you? You see, there is a dynamic and a value to "changeability" that must be examined. I'm not referring to "change" for the sake of change. I'm referring to the kind of "change" which is necessary and intrinsically valuable for our own growth and development.

Why is this important? It's important because sometimes we can become complacent with the status quo. It's important because sometimes you can become dull. It's important because sometimes I can lose the dynamic of life and become lethargic. "We've always done it this way before" becomes our life's motto. New and innovative ways are never even attempted, and we soon fall behind the power curve.

In fact, change can be healthy and good for us if we approach it with the proper attitude. Change, properly approached, can bring about new opportunities, great wonders and even great miracles in our lives. Since change is an integral part of life I must identify the element that brings stability amid flux and here it is:

"Jesus (God) is the same yesterday and today and forever."

Because of God's reliability during my instability I can still progress in a positive manner. I can learn how not to fight or resist change but learn to rejoice in it because God, who is unchanging, becomes the point of stability in my world.

It would follow that my capacity to change is indicative of the quality of my faith in God. Why? Because I know that in God's own unchanging nature, He is in control of all the change going on around me and will use change to shape and mature my life. Growth is essential, and change will bring personal growth as we use each experience in life as an object lesson.

⁘ *Commit to the LORD whatever you do, and your plans will succeed.*

*(Proverbs 16:3)*

## FOR THE GRADUATE

DR. SEUSS HAS written and illustrated over forty books for children (of all ages) and their very fortunate parents. One of those books written in the early 1990's became a national bestseller. I believe you can still find it in bookstores.

The book *OH, The Places You'll Go!* is a compilation of rhyme verses giving advice to children on how to proceed in life when confronting the sometimes inevitable experiences of fear, loneliness and confusion. The invaluable advice is given with a view towards preparing children to face and surmount those common human predicaments. Here's a brief excerpt:

*"Out there things can happen*    *All alone!*
*And frequently do*    *Whether you like it or not,*
*To people as brainy*    *Alone will be something*
*And footsy as you*    *You'll be quite a lot*

*And when you're alone, there's a very good chance you'll meet things that scare you right out of your pants. There and some, down the road between hither and yon, that can scare you so much you won't want to go on...."* (*OH, The Places You'll Go!* Dr. Seuss. Random House, N.Y. 1990)

And, if you would indulge me with my own addition: "You'll know the hard places. You'll know the lonely places." These are words of warning and wisdom for those who will listen and are most especially suited for the countless thousands who yearly graduate from our nation's schools.

Dr. Seuss' book can be a timely gift item for our children as well as school graduates (of all ages) traversing that yearly rite of passage we call commencement exercises. As parents we share a reasonable concern for the safety of our kids. We would like to shelter our children from the difficulties of life. But, we are also aware that it is impossible to shelter our children from those hard places and lonely places. However, what we can do is teach our children in the way they should go. As responsible parents we can practice some preventive medicine and equip our kids with the necessary tools for making the right decisions. When life isn't fair and when facing those mountains of desperation how can our children stand on solid ground?

From another book, written long ago in a land far away, comes timeless wisdom that is foundational to standing on solid ground. The advice was given to a warrior preparing to lead a people into unknown territory. Indeed, he was facing one of those dark and lonely places in life. Joshua, a man in his middle years, receives three invaluable axioms for living that are just as applicable today and worthy of transmitting to our children.

> AXIOM 1: BE STRONG AND COURAGEOUS. *Being strong and courageous is right if it is not an arrogant type of courage. It is also right if it is not dismissive of God's providential presence. Being strong and courageous must come from knowing the character and the wisdom of God. I can have a sense of inner peace and confidence, not because I am tough but because my God has the track record of performance. Yes, our children will have to face those hard places in life that will demand strength and courage. Let us ensure that they know the eternal source of strength and courage.*

> AXIOM 2: LET GOD'S WORDS BE YOUR WORDS. *This is a critical element in arming our kids to face a cynical world. Indeed, the Holy Scriptures are filled with the wisdom of the ages. Neither all the collective brilliance of mankind nor all of the atheistic minds in history have ever destroyed its veracity. If its wisdom can permeate our children's thoughts and their words, then they will be standing on a firm foundation.*

Axiom 3: God will never leave you. *One day
my children will face tough choices. They may be
tempted to succumb to peer-pressure; they may fear
the future or face loneliness. The reality is that we are
never alone. Indeed, my children's faith will be tem-
pered and strengthened as they affirm the presence
of God amid their struggle.*

"And will you succeed?
Yes! You will, indeed! …
KID, YOU'LL MOVE THE MOUNTAINS!" (*OH, The Places
You'll Go!*)

⟊ *Now we know that if the earthly tent we live in
is destroyed, we have a building from God, an
eternal house in heaven, not built by human
hands.*

*(2 Corinthians 5:1)*

## One Day to Live

I must take you back in history a little but…there it was! Right
before my eyes: "The death of Superman" …POW!…ZAP!…
KAPUT! The man of steel was no longer. I was looking at the last
issue of Superman comics. I once though that this day would never
come up. I once fantasized that my kids, and maybe grandkids,
would also relish in Superman's victories over Lex Luthor and other
villainous characters. According to the last issue of "Superman" the

much-revered superhero was done-in by the likes of the crazed escapee from a galactic insane asylum. His name: "Doomsday."

But what was it that really destroyed superman? Well, it was a combination of the times and economics. Superman's time had run out. His technology was outdated and no longer in demand by the public. The "coup de grace" came in November 1992 when D.C. Comics sold the last single issue of "Superman."

The demise of the superhero reminds us of a very simple verity about life:

- Everyone will have their last day.

- Everyone's time will come up, sooner or later.

I know that time is a valuable commodity to us. I sense it as I see humanity hustle and bustle up and down the corridors of corporate America. There is a great sense of urgency and focus as we conduct our business. The demeanor and determination that our society is known for endeavors to make the best use of the day before it runs out of time.

If Superman knew that he only had one more day to live before encountering "Doomsday" how would he have lived his last twenty-four hours? What about us? How differently would we live our lives if we only had twenty-four more hours of life? For us, the question is pregnant with significance. The question is fraught with serious implications. Indeed, if we were to seriously think about "time" we might agree that time is an education in eternity. Consider this: In "time" God has given us a slice of His eternity. As such let us consider a simple formula for being good stewards of this valuable temporal commodity:

1. LIVE WISELY: Make the most of every opportunity because our time evaporates before us. What we do with it today will determine how our tomorrows will turn out. When we live wisely we are putting first things first and not allowing the minor details to dominate and drive the really important things. Take care of your "today" for it will determine how your "tomorrow" is lived.

2. LIVE WORSHIPFULLY: Living worshipfully is predicated by our sense of personal relationship with God. When we are sensitive to the Almighty we will be truly alive and sensitive to our surroundings. We will develop a tolerant heart because we'll understand the intolerant times in which we live. We will understand each other's eternal values before the Creator. We will make of our lives an expression of worship.

3. LIVE THANKFULLY: Let us thank God for the simple things such as:

   - A smile from your child/ an expression of encouragement from a friend.
   - A place to call home/ a place of worship/ people you can trust.
   - A beautiful day/ God's benevolent provisions.

Are we living wisely? Are we living worshipfully? Are we living thankfully?

Here's one more timeless reminder: "Take good care of your future, because that's where you're going to spend the rest of your life." (C.F. Kettering)

Let's live as though we have one more day to live!

·✠· *For I know the plans I have for you, declares the LORD, plans to prosper you and not to harm you, plans to give you hope and a future.*
*(Jeremiah 29:11)*

## GAINING A FOCUS ON THE FUTURE

As I THINK about the future my thoughts take me to a famous painting created by Titian, a 16th century Venetian artist. Titian created a work known as "An Allegory of Prudence." The artist desired to communicate what it means to be prudent. Titian portrayed prudence as a man with three heads. One head was of a youth, confidently facing the future. Another head was that of a mature man eyeing the present, with all its responsibilities. The third head was that of a wise, elderly man gazing at the past with a great expression of nostalgia on his face. He was fondly reminiscing his glory days of youth and energy. Over their heads Titian wrote a Latin phrase that when translated read: "From the example of the past, the man of the present acts prudently so as not to imperil the future." I am happy to report that I rarely perceive myself as a man with three heads, but the object lesson of the painting is very clear.

The essence of the painting's meaning addresses gaining a focus (a balanced focus) on the future. We need that kind of wisdom today as we face the future together. That kind of wisdom must prevail if we are to rise above anxieties produced by past failures and the fear of repeating those mistakes in the future. This type of anxiety will keep us from enjoying life in the present and properly planning for the future.

Let's face it. The future can be scary to think about. The great unknown can leave too many questions unanswered. We may plan "theoretically" knowing that those plans can be changed through a simple twist of fate. But still, we must face the future and deal with the important questions: What is my focus on the future? How far ahead can I see? Do I have a vision for life?

Indeed, the strength of my life is dependent on gaining and maintaining that proper focus. It is found that those who have a clear concentration on the future are most fruitful and most flexible. How then can we effectively gain that proper focus? I submit to you three easily identifiable pointers that begin with two simple words, "Let us."

1.  LET US DRAW NEAR TO GOD: To do so is to gain confidence in our lives. To do so is to gain a focus on the future. Not to do so is to miss out on a great life adventure. As we intentionally decide to seek God's Grace, great things begin to happen. We will become immersed in a vision for good, sound and balanced living. It is living in a type of victory that is perennial and life giving. We will become less focused on the demands of "religion" and more focused on a living relationship with the Almighty.

2.  LET US HOLD ON TO OUR HOPE: Hope is not wishful thinking. It is a full assurance in the sovereignty and goodness of God. Hope is not compromise. Rather, hope is persevering. My hope

needs to be foundational to my faith. It doesn't bend or yield to the blowing winds of temptation, convenience or circumstances. Hope holds firm to what is essential to my integrity. Hope is the stuff of which martyrs have given their lives for. Chances are that you and I will never have to be martyred for the hope that we have. But, we can live for our families, our faith and our commitments in hope.

3. LET US CONSIDER AND ENCOURAGE ONE ANOTHER: this is otherwise known as "building community." This means that we build understanding in a relationship of mutual responsibility. Mutual consideration and encouragement are fostered as people go beyond just being courteous and actually commit to each other. The ancient Greeks had a word for this, "koinonia" which meant "community," "fellowship." This requires that people risk for each other and assume responsibility for each other.

We stand on the threshold of a future filled with unknown possibilities and great potential for good. Let us live prudently and learn from the mistakes of the past so as to make wise decisions in the present and not endanger the future.

# Scripture Index

# About the Author

D R. JOE (JOSE) R. Molina is an ordained Baptist Minister. After several years of pastoral ministries in the South Florida area Joe was endorsed and commissioned as a United States Navy Chaplain. After serving on active duty, Commander Molina, (USN, UMSC) was selected as the 11th Chaplain to the Corps of Cadets and Director of Religious Activities at The Citadel (The Military College of South Carolina), Charleston, where he resides with his wife Vicky and Maggie, the American Dingo. They have two grown sons, Thomas and Daniel.

He holds the Bachelor of Arts from Long Island University, the Master of Divinity from New Orleans Baptist Theological Seminary, The Education Specialist degree from Liberty University and a Doctor of Ministry degree from Luther Rice Seminary.

OTHER PUBLISHED WORK: *The Homiletic Methods of John of Antioch (Chrysostom) and Augustine of Hippo as a Paradigm for Postmodern Preaching.*

> http://www.worldcat.org/title/homiletic-methods-of-john-of-antioch-chrysostom-and-augustine-of-hippo-as-a-paradigm-for-postmodern-preaching/oclc/919980176ß

Made in United States
Orlando, FL
22 November 2021